THE
SPIRIT'S WAY
HOME

About the Author

Natalie Fowler is a published author of both fiction and non-fiction paranormal works. She is a regular contributor and staff editor for FATE, the longest-running print paranormal news magazine featuring stories of the strange and unknown. Natalie is also a paranormal investigator for Ghost Stories Ink. As an avid researcher with a passion for history, she serves as the group's historian. With Ghost Stories Ink, she has conducted paranormal investigations across the country, from LA to Manhattan. As a practicing psychic medium, Natalie helps clients access their Akashic records, meet their spirit guides and angels, and connect with loved ones who have passed. In her clearing work, Natalie has a gift for connecting with those spirits who need their stories understood. Recently, she co-founded Paranormal Services Cooperative to promote and encourage paranormal unity and to offer education and assistance with respect to spirit rescue. She lives in St. Paul, Minnesota, with her family.

To learn more about Natalie's other works and projects, please visit her website at www.NatalieFowler.com.

THE
SPIRIT'S WAY
HOME

Inspiring Stories
from a
Psychic
Medium

Natalie Fowler

Llewellyn Publications
Woodbury, Minnesota

FIRST EDITION
First Printing, 2020

Book design by Samantha Peterson
Cover design by Shannon McKuhen

Llewellyn Publications is a registered trademark of Llewellyn Worldwide Ltd.

Library of Congress Cataloging-in-Publication Data
Names: Fowler, Natalie (Paranormal investigator), author.
Title: The spirit's way home : inspiring stories from a psychic medium / by
    Natalie Fowler.
Description: First edition. | Woodbury, MN : Llewellyn Publications, [2020]
    | Summary: "The Spirit's Way Home gives you a deeper understanding of
    spirits and their powerful stories of love, loss, and hope. This moving
    and emotional book is a testament to the power of psychic communication
    and human compassion" —Provided by publisher.
Identifiers: LCCN 2020025348 (print) | LCCN 2020025349 (ebook) | ISBN
    9780738765310 (paperback) | ISBN 9780738765976 (ebook)
Subjects: LCSH: Fowler, Natalie (Paranormal investigator) | Women
    psychics—United States—Biography. | Women mediums—United
    States—Biography. | Psychic ability. | Ghosts. | Spirits. | Parapsychology.
Classification: LCC BF1027.F68 A3 2020 (print) | LCC BF1027.F68 (ebook)
    | DDC 133.9092 [B]—dc23
LC record available at https://lccn.loc.gov/2020025348
LC ebook record available at https://lccn.loc.gov/2020025349

Llewellyn Publications
A Division of Llewellyn Worldwide Ltd.
2143 Wooddale Drive
Woodbury, MN 55125-2989
www.llewellyn.com

Printed in the United States of America

To Mac and Megan

CONTENTS

ACKNOWLEDGMENTS

Thank you to my husband, John, for your unending patience and support when I announce that I am going off on yet another weekend adventure or paranormal investigation, and for supporting my "sorcery." To my kids, Avery, Luke, and Isabelle, for teaching me so much and embracing the crazy in their mother.

To my father for telling me there were a lot of things I could do with a law degree (even if this wasn't what you had in mind when you said it). To my mother for having the courage to pursue her own healing gifts—and for the pendulum help when mine doesn't work. And to my mother-in-law, Susan Fowler, for your unending support.

Thank you to my agent and friend, Dawn Fredericks. Your "Tweet Up" Happy Hours are brilliant and I will be forever grateful.

Thank you to the entire staff at Llewellyn who helped make this the best book it could be, especially Amy Glaser and Nicole Borneman.

Thank you to my soul sister, Jessica Freeburg, for introducing me to a whole new world and for inviting me along on some amazing adventures. Thank you to my Ghost Stories Ink family.

Kelley Freese, Beth Bock, and Kelley Erickson, you are the three wise sisters I got to choose. I love you all. 11:11.

Thank you to the Palmer House Hotel and its amazing staff on both sides of the veil. You teach me lessons at every turn and it has been an honor. Jenny Melton, I can't wait for the next adventure.

Thank you to the entire staff at Forepaugh's Restaurant, but especially Mimi, Ben, George, and Molly.

Thank you to my PSC team for sharing my passion and mission. To Kevin Swanson, for using the words "spirit rescue" and for trying to teach me about all of the equipment. To Nicole, for seeing the things that I cannot and for listening to me talk everything through, sometimes in excess. I'm grateful to have found you both.

To all of my mentors, for doing what you do and teaching me what you know, especially: Annette Bruchu, Jenny Canfield, Lisa Eckman, Maureen Higgins, and Suzanne Worthley. Thank you for being you and doing what you do.

Thank you to Sally and Jesseca for being my biggest fans and always reading anything I throw at you.

Thank you to Meredith for moving to 555, for accepting this Cancer, and for Capricorning the s#!t out of everything we do together.

Last, but certainly not least, thank you to my spirit guides and angels for always being there for me.

INTRODUCTION

When I was about twelve or thirteen years old, I was afraid to go to sleep in my own room. There was a dark shadow that I swore was watching me from the corner. Whenever I mentioned it to anyone, I was told over and over again that it was just my imagination. I was told that there was no such thing as ghosts. Eventually, I began to believe that. I *wanted* to believe that because I had no idea what to do about it otherwise—the alternative was too overwhelming.

But somewhere deep down, I must have known that ghosts were very real. Because even though everyone was telling me they didn't exist, I still wanted to know more. I was fascinated by ghosts. More than anything, I wanted to know their stories. Why were they here? Were they stuck? If so, why? How did they get stuck? Were they afraid to be a ghost? Did they wish they could find some help?

My life ended up taking a practical route. I graduated from law school and went on to practice at a small firm. I loved studying the law. I thrived with a good research and writing project, but I hated private practice. I made a terrible attorney—I figured out (the hard way) that confrontation made me cry. That realization helped me find my way into the world of legal publishing; I was much happier at a desk with a stack of laws that needed sorting and editing than I was on the phone or in court with angry attorneys. Looking back now with the knowledge and understanding that I am an empath, it's no wonder I struggled as an attorney.

In the meantime, one of my creative ideas had started to bubble to fruition. I invented a character who was trained to think logically and rationally (like a lawyer) and gave her something completely irrational and inexplicable to deal with (like a ghost). I started writing paranormal mystery novels.

Not long after, my own children were old enough to start talking about the shadows in the corner that they were seeing, sensing, and feeling. As someone who was researching, studying, and writing about ghosts, I could hardly tell them that there was no such thing. I was not going to tell them that "it was just their imagination." I knew I needed to come up with something better.

Little did I know that the universe had an interesting plan for me. My own psychic gifts began to wake up. Now I know that those shadows in my room were real. Now I know the reasons they get stuck. I also know how to help them. This is my story . . . but more importantly, it's theirs.

ONE
WHAT DO YOU MEAN
I'M PSYCHIC?

"Isabelle, let's go. We're going to be late," I said to my seven-year-old daughter. Actually, *we* weren't going to be late, *I* was going to be late for my scheduled phone call if we didn't pick it up a little. We pushed through the door of the ice arena and within a few minutes, her skates were tied, she had her punch card in hand, and she was waiting patiently for her teacher.

I gave her a kiss on the top of her blond head. "Have a good lesson. I'll be back in when I'm done."

"Okay Mommy," she said.

I hurried back out to the car, took a deep breath, situated myself, and waited for my phone to read 6:30 p.m. My heart beat just a little faster in my chest. I'd only done this twice before, and both times the information I'd gotten was incredibly insightful and valuable. I'd gotten a lot of direction about the manuscripts I'd been working on, both of which were now in the hands of my literary agent. I had figured I could use some good news about my books, so I tried not to think too much about the money I'd spent on the scheduled phone call I was about to make.

When the minutes flipped from 29 to 30, I dialed the number for the psychic my best friend, Jessica, had recommended. She answered on the second ring and my psychic reading officially began.

"I believe we all have spirit guides who help us through our lives. I talk to them to help you—" she started to explain but then stopped. "Wait. Never mind. Your guide is telling me to skip over this part and just get on with it. You already know what this sort of thing is all about and how it works."

I smiled to myself. The first time I'd ever had a reading with a psychic, my guide had butted right past hers to just talk to her directly. Apparently, that wasn't how it usually worked for her. It was comforting to know his behavior was consistent.

"He's got a whole list of things that we need to talk about. In fact," she said, "he's carrying a clipboard."

That made me smile again. "Yep. That sounds like him."

"We're starting with the biggest thing on his list," she said. "You're an empath."

"I'm a what?" I asked.

"An empath," she repeated. "You're a psychic."

"What do you mean I'm a psychic?" I asked, but I didn't wait for her to continue. "I guess I've always been really intuitive, but I wouldn't call myself psychic."

"You should," she said. "It's much more than just your intuition. You're actually really psychic—more than you give yourself credit for. In fact, you've actually been reading for your friends your entire life but you've never called it that. You just seem to always know the perfect thing to tell them."

The last part, at least, was true. People always called on me for advice. And I always seemed to just somehow know what to tell them.

"Eventually, you'll be doing readings for others and you'll be charging for them."

I laughed out loud. "I don't know about that. I'm an introverted author who prefers dark corners and creepy basements."

"Just you wait," she said.

I had no idea in that moment how much my life would start to shift and change.

By this time, I was already writing ghost stories. I had also joined a group that took a different approach to the idea of a ghost hunt. Ghost Stories Ink is a group of authors and illustrators who go on paranormal investigations in search of creative inspiration. It wasn't so much about finding "proof" that ghosts existed, but rather, letting your creepy surroundings inspire your art and craft.

But I had never intended to go looking for ghosts—my group found me. My friend Jessica was the founder of Ghost Stories Ink. One night, she invited me to go along on a paranormal investigation. They were going to investigate a private residence that was rumored to be haunted ... and they would be filming for their documentary.

I was terrified. I'd been researching and writing about ghosts for years, but I wasn't sure if I really wanted to go shake one out of an attic. But even more so, I was an introvert who was terrified about being filmed during my first ghost hunt. I didn't want to look stupid.

I agreed to go anyway. To prepare, I did what I do best: I went to the library and stuck my nose in a book. I researched. I ended up finding all sorts of juicy details to talk about, from obituaries to scintillating newspaper articles about a long-ago homeowner from the residence we would be investigating. I might not know the first thing about ghost-hunting tools, but my research-geek, nerdy self was armed with something even better—information.

I must have had enough to talk about and I must not have looked too stupid because the day after the ghost hunt, I was invited to join the group as their researcher and historian. We've since been on coast-to-coast ghost hunts from LA to Manhattan. This soccer mom suddenly found herself traveling to Los Angeles with her paranormal investigative group wearing a backpack filled with ghost-hunting equipment. Who wouldn't laugh when the security guard asked, "You're going where? To do what?" My life had taken an unbelievably cool turn.

The stage was already set. My extracurricular activities connected me to the spirit world in an unusual way. Now that I was armed with the knowledge that I was "psychic," everything was about to shift into fast forward.

———————

I took my psychic reading seriously. I spent the next few days processing. I read, I learned, and I meditated. I found mentors. I started taking classes—for myself this time, not just to learn for the sake of my characters.

I searched for definitions of "empath." When I found one, I could certainly relate. I was absolutely someone who took on other people's emotions as my own. I realized I *was* intuiting psychic information through the emotions and feelings of others. It felt like a special puzzle piece had finally clicked into place.

I'd always been comfortable calling myself intuitive, but I wasn't sure if I could wrap my head around being psychic. Merriam-Webster defines intuition as "quick and ready insight," "immediate apprehension or cognition," and "the power ... of attaining to direct knowledge or cognition without evident rational thought."[1] According to this definition, the dictionary seems to define intuition as psychic.

But "without evident rational thought" was not necessarily something that was part of my vocabulary. I am a trained attorney. I've been trained to prove points with facts and supporting precedent. I loved law school. I thrived in that sort of academic environment. I wasn't ready to let go of evident rational thought, no matter how psychic I was told I was.

Through my reading and study I learned about the different psychic gifts. I eventually figured out that for me, my gift of clairvoyance works mostly in my mind's eye. I have the ability

• • • • • • • • • • • •

1. *Merriam-Webster*, s.v. "intuition," accessed March 3, 2020, https://www.merriam
-webster.com/dictionary/intuition.

to "see" images in my third eye. When I close my eyes in a meditative state, I can see my guides, images of people, places, lost items … whatever psychic information my guides think I need to know.

I am an incredibly creative person; I had always thought the images I've been seeing in my head my whole life were just coming from my imagination. But I've come to realize that my imagination is actually the bridge to my psychic abilities. As I began to develop my psychic gifts, it became important to me to find ways to validate the psychic information I was receiving and to learn to discern what was coming in as psychic information and what might be my imagination.

Most often, the voice inside my head is my own. I talk to myself in my head all day long with a random running dialogue of observations and opinions. But as I studied the different psychic gifts and learned more about clairaudience—the gift of "hearing" or the ability to obtain psychic information through an ability to hear things others cannot—I realized that sometimes the information I was hearing inside my head was not actually resonating from me, even though I was hearing it in my own voice.

I began to discern that sometimes, this voice—my voice— was actually giving me guidance. For example, I often heard it when walking through the grocery store. Random grocery items popped in my head as I walked through the aisles. I realized I hadn't used a list at the grocery store in years. I began to acknowledge that my guides were actually yelling out the items on a list they were keeping for me. To this day, they still make sure I don't forget any groceries.

I've even had arguments with myself at the grocery store. I will get a nudge or hear the voice inside my head say something like, "You need almonds."

To which I reply (in my head), "No, I bought almonds last week."

And the voice in my head repeats, "You need to buy almonds."

Sometimes I listen, sometimes I don't. When I don't—and I get home to find out that someone ate all of the almonds I had planned to use in the salad I wanted to make—it validates the voice in my head that told me I should have bought more.

Another one of the psychic gifts is clairsentience. Clairsentience is the ability to receive psychic information through the sense of touch or feeling. It is the ability to feel the energy from others physically. Energy practitioners, like Reiki masters or Healing Touch providers, physically feel energy with their hands. Sometimes my hands buzz. This is something I'm trying to develop further.

But clairsentience is also the ability to feel the emotions emanating from others. This is the most common of the psychic gifts, and it describes those who identify with being an empath. It can also be the most troublesome.

If an empath doesn't know they are picking up on the emotions of others, that empath can suddenly be experiencing the feelings and emotions of those around them. It's like getting on a roller coaster of high and low mood swings that we didn't even know we'd agreed to go on (because we actually didn't).

At the moment I learned and acknowledged I was a clairsentient empath, my life made more sense. It changed the way I related and interacted with my own family. (Mostly because I was more careful to start discerning which emotions were mine and which ones might be coming from someone else.)

I also have the gift of claircognizance, or the ability to just know something is true. For me, this is the strongest of my psychic gifts. It is also the most troublesome for my logical lawyer brain because it is psychic information coming in without any substantiating fact. There is not a voice that says it; there is not a picture that accompanies it; it is simply a piece of information that resonates from somewhere deep within and I just know because I *know*.

Over time, I've learned to discern that this information resonates from a different part of me than my brain: it comes from my solar plexus. It's that gut feeling that tells me something is true.

Realizing and finally acknowledging these gifts within myself and identifying how they worked for me felt like I'd finally found a piece of my soul I never knew had been missing.

But as a trained attorney, all of it presented a challenge. As a logical person who prefers to be able to prove things with facts, embracing these gifts and actually using them for whatever the universe had in mind was not going to be easy. I wasn't sure if I would be able to find a way to make these two polar-opposite sides of myself work together. It certainly was going to take some time to figure out.

But this was me. This was who I was. It was such a relief to finally know. And yet, it created a whole new question ... What the heck was I supposed to do with this "gift"?

It didn't take too long to figure it out, and the answer surprised me. Once, when I was almost completely alone at the Palmer House (a haunted hotel in Sauk Centre, Minnesota) a ghost called me the "Story Lady." I often get downloads of stories about the ghosts that I help. And yet, the logical lawyer in me is constantly looking for ways to "prove" that this is more than just my imagination. I've researched to validate some of it. I've reasoned through other parts. Paranormal evidence like EVPs and SLS imaging can be undeniable proof that reinforces my downloads.

To say I've learned a lot is an understatement. I've accidentally brought ghosts home with me. My family has learned a lot, whether they wanted to or not. The last time I had one follow me home, after I had sent it on its way and confessed its presence to everyone in my house, the kids rolled their eyes and said, "Oh Mom. You have to do better about that."

I'm a psychic work in progress. And it all began with someone I knew from high school. She was an acquaintance, and her name was Megan. With her help, I was about to learn very quickly what I was going to be doing with my newly discovered gifts.

Megan

About six months after my reading, a woman I knew from high school passed away. It wasn't unexpected to those who knew her well, but it was a surprise to me.

I learned that she passed thanks to a vague social media post made by a mutual acquaintance who instructed her to "rest in

peace." I was shocked. I knew she'd been sick, but I hadn't realized death was imminent. Sally, my best friend from high school,
had been friends with her as an adult. I wanted to pass along my
condolences, and I knew she'd be able to answer the questions
generated by the vague post.

After hearing the story and details, I felt bad that someone
had posted about her death on social media. I realized Megan's
close friends were trying hard to respect her privacy.

The next night, at 3:00 a.m., I woke up and couldn't get back
to sleep. As I lay there, I got an image in my head of Megan.

"You need to f*&*ing tell me about heaven," she said.
"What do you know about it?"

Surprised, I thought for a minute and wondered if I was
dreaming. I wasn't about to talk out loud to something I wasn't
even sure was there. Also, my husband was asleep next to me,
and I didn't want to wake him up ... or confuse him.

In my head I answered, "It's a loving, forgiving place."

Megan was quiet, and in that moment I got an instant
download of a story—it was as if someone had just stuck a
flash drive in me and gave me access to information I hadn't
known. That download caused me to add to my answer, "You
don't need to see anyone you don't want to see when you go
to heaven."

"I don't f&^%ing believe you," she said.

"If you go," I continued in my head, "you can come back
and see anyone you want here on Earth at any time. You can
still be with your loved ones here."

"F*&%ing A," she answered. "I don't believe you."

"If you go, you can come back, and then you'll be better able to help them. It will be hard to help them if you stay."

And then she disappeared … leaving me to stare at my ceiling for the next hour thinking, *That was weird*, and wondering, *Did I just make that up?*

I finally fell asleep after convincing myself that my active mystery-writer brain was on overdrive, and my imagination must have been fueled by the way the news of her death had been shared.

But just in case, the next day, I called my friend Sally to ask if Megan swore a lot.

She laughed and said, "Every other word was the f-bomb."

Huh.

I explained what happened and why I was asking, and her conclusion was that it definitely sounded like Megan.

Two days later, I was in the midst of a battle with my youngest after school. She was throwing a fit about having to do her homework. She is my spicy child and any battle of wills requires as much patience as I can manage.

Depleted, I put myself in time-out and went out to sit on the backyard patio step until I could calm down and pull myself together. I needed to sort through my own emotions and make sure I didn't explode a pile of ick onto my youngest child when I went back inside.

Out of nowhere, Megan was there again. I felt her presence and she sat down next to me.

"My family is driving me f*&#ing nuts."

"Seriously?" I asked. "I'm in the middle of a tantrum about homework and you want to do this now?"

She ignored me. But in the back of my mind, I realized that I was not and could not be making this up. Here I was sitting there on that step, focusing all of my time, energy, and effort to calm myself down and find my patience. Never in a million years would I be having this conversation with Megan right here, right now if it was just my imagination at play. All of my energy and attention was on my family back inside.

I wasn't sure if she could hear my inner dialogue. If she could, she ignored it. Megan explained she was tired of her family talking about her death and trying to plan her funeral. "Are you telling me the truth about not having to see anyone I don't want to see?"

"Of course. Heaven can be whatever you want it to be."

"I'm still not f&%^ing sure if I believe you."

And then I had a thought. If Megan didn't believe me, maybe she'd believe Mac. After all, he had firsthand experience.

Mac was a mutual friend of ours. He was also my husband's best friend, and he had died six years after we'd all graduated from high school—he was murdered when someone broke into his home. My husband and I had actually reunited at Mac's funeral and started dating. We were engaged one year later on the anniversary of his death so the day would stand for something good too. I've often felt his presence around us throughout the years. He especially likes our middle son, Luke. More than once, I've whispered a prayer to Mac, asking if he could keep an eye on our adventurous middle child.

So I asked Mac to come. I explained that Megan didn't believe me about heaven and asked if he could come help me out. He was there in an instant.

I don't even think it took any words. Upon seeing him, Megan was ready to go and off they went. I'm assuming toward a light, but I didn't see where.

That left me with nothing to do but go back in the house and deal with the temper tantrum still raging inside.

Looking back, I know I didn't make this all up. If I had, I would have made the ending much more dramatic. Angels would have been singing and lights would have been shining bright. Instead, they simply went off together somewhere and I didn't even see where.

Megan showed up for me again a few months later, in July. I was out at happy hour with two of her close friends. Somehow, the three of us had all gotten stuck planning our high school reunion.

I was about to leave, but there was Megan standing behind me. "You can't leave until you tell Bridgit that I am here."

In my head I said, "But I've never told them that I can talk to dead people."

"I don't care. You need to tell her," she said.

I rolled my eyes and took a deep breath. "This is going to sound a little crazy," I told the two living women in front of me. They both looked at me expectantly. "Um. Megan's here, and she really wants Bridgit to know how grateful she is for everything you did for her in the end."

Bridgit burst into tears. She told me that she was carrying a lot of guilt about some of the decisions they'd had to make in the end. We talked for a few minutes about that difficult time. I'm not even sure if I shared with them the story about how Megan showed up for me in the days that followed after she passed. Maybe I did, only because it would help explain why Megan was standing there now. I know I remember feeling like I didn't want any of it to be about me.

But I was grateful I'd found the courage to share at least some of the crazy that was going on in my head. After, when I was driving home, I realized I should have asked Megan to show me something only Bridgit would know about.

The second the question was formed in my head, I got the image of Megan holding a bright, reddish-orange flower. Maybe a Gerbera daisy? I have no idea what it means and I've never had the chance to ask Bridgit about it. It's not exactly the sort of thing you can call someone up and ask about over the phone.

But if I were to call Bridgit on the phone, I would tell her that Megan loves to pop in on her and her daughter, especially when they go to the park. She is also watching closely over her nieces and loves them dearly.

Megan has become a good friend to me. She's someone I've been able to call on for help. It is indescribably special to be able to say you know someone better in death than you knew them in life.

Megan was the first soul I helped find her way to where she was supposed to go. And I am incredibly blessed to consider her a friend. With her help, I learned that I would be using my gifts to help lost souls cross over and find their way to heaven.

My Spirit Guides

Part of working to develop my gifts has been to get to know my spirit guides. I have one guide who has been with me since birth. He's a little pushy. The first time I ever had a psychic reading, my guide shoved past the psychic's guides to talk to her directly. He was obviously excited for the opportunity to talk to me.

Over the last few years, I've tried to get to know him better. I started to realize how very protective he was the first time I went on a paranormal investigation with my Ghost Stories Ink group. I remember going into the house and I could feel his nervousness. It was a small house, and now that I know more about what I'm doing, looking back, I've realized there was something really icky in the basement.

That was my first paranormal investigation and the only time I've been on an investigation where we didn't get a single piece of evidence or have a single experience that could even remotely be classified as paranormal. I remember driving home with the overwhelming sensation that it was my fault nothing happened. My guide was working so hard to protect me, he protected everyone in the group and nothing happened.

Not long after, I got a download of information about my guide. In his last life, he was in protective services—probably for the Italian Mafia. But every time I mention that to anyone, he yells really loudly, "But I never killed anyone."

The very next day, I was headed to my second paranormal investigation (the group was filming for our documentary and our director was in town). My intuition on the drive to the location didn't work at all. I can usually find my way relatively easily, instinctively knowing when to turn and where to go. Instead, I got really lost. I had none of the usual pulls to turn left or right and ended up miles from my destination. I gave up and turned on my GPS and had a really good conversation with my guide.

He explained that he was trying to demonstrate what it felt like not to have guidance by not helping me find my destination. He explained that if I was going to do this sort of work, I had to trust him. If he told me not to go somewhere, I absolutely had to listen. I agreed. He advised me not to go back to that first house ever again. He also won't let me go to the Villisca Axe Murder House (which is fine by me).

He doesn't always know what to do with a girl. My grandmother shows up quite often to help out with any "girl" stuff. My grandmother and I were very close. I used to visit her by myself for a week every summer when I was a little girl and it was always the highlight of my summer. I spent a lot of time with her before she passed away. I always suspected she would keep an eye on me from heaven, but now I know exactly how true that really is.

When my boys were little, my husband and I moved to Belgium. We lived there as expats for six years. Our daughter was born there. When we moved back to the United States, I had a very difficult time with the transition and slipped into a depression. My heart was broken and I had to go through an entire grieving process as we reacclimated to our own culture.

One night I was sitting in my room praying for help. I could see my guide (although, at the time, I didn't know too much about him yet) and he threw up his arms as if to say, "I've got nothing. I don't know what to do."

In that very moment, I felt both of my grandmothers arrive as if they were each their own ball of light. They landed, one on each side of me. They stayed with me just like that (one on each side) for a long time afterward. They were with me until I had completely gone through my grieving process.

My Grandma Rita is still around quite often. I especially feel her presence when I am cooking. My Grandma Eileen was quite stylish. I often feel her presence when I'm shopping. I can feel her distaste if I pull something off the rack that's not quite my color or style.

———————

As I began doing this sort of work, I had a few new guides join me. One of them is a bit ... unorthodox. He showed up for me after I had a very nasty incident with a treadmill. A few winters ago, I drove a car full of thirteen-year-olds to a soccer tournament in Kansas City. Our first morning, I woke up early to sneak in a run in the hotel workout room. After all, I was going to have to sit in a gym all day watching futsal games (a version of indoor soccer).

The hotel was filled with tournament teams and other parents in charge of preteen and teenage kids with early schedules. The tiny workout room was packed, but there was one empty treadmill left. I hopped on, started my music, and set my pace. Within a few minutes, my headphones became tangled and

I did something that no one should ever do on a treadmill: I stopped.

It was an out-of-body experience. I seemed to watch in slow motion as my body crumpled, fell, and shot backward off the machine and became a pile on the floor. Stunned, I sat for a minute trying to assess the damage. Every single person in the room got off their machine to check on me. Which was all very kind and good of them, but I was mortified.

I stood up and stretched. I had a weird rubber burn that ran the entire length of my leg. But I could move every limb and none of it seemed to be too terrible. I considered myself lucky. I realized I had two choices. I could slink out the door and go back to my room. Or I could try to salvage something from my workout and get back on.

Not one to back down from a challenge, I got back on. I don't think anyone even noticed when I reset the length of my run and nearly cut it in half. Except for the weird rubber burn which took a few weeks to heal, everything seemed fine and good.

Until about six weeks later when I woke up and could barely get out of bed because my back hurt so bad. I'd never experienced anything like it. For the first time in my life, I found a chiropractor and scheduled multiple massages in a row. I was forced into self-care, something I still have to consciously remember.

A friend of mine practices shamanic massage. Every time I've gone to see her, cool stuff happens. She is incredibly psychic, so she always gets messages and images that pop in and out while she is working. After, we talk about the different downloads and try to put the information together. She is especially tuned in to the inner-earth energies and spirit animals.

During my session with her, something new showed up for me. He wasn't like anyone—or any *thing*—I'd ever seen before. He stood there with his arms crossed. His pose reminded me of the Teenage Mutant Ninja Turtles. In fact, everything about him looked like a Teenage Mutant Ninja Turtle . . . except instead of a turtle, he was a beetle. His back was protected by a special shell, yet he walked upright like a human. He didn't say anything at all. I just knew he was for me, and I knew he wasn't going anywhere. But I didn't know exactly what I was supposed to do with him.

It was in this moment and through this experience that I realized our spirit guides could come from places other than just the earth's dimension. We can have guides from anywhere, from any plane of existence (and there are several).

I grew up believing in angels. I can see, sense, and feel they are there. If angels (from the divine realm) are present to assist us in our daily lives and work, my logical brain accepted the possibility that there could be guides and assistants from other realms as well. We just might not know what they all are.

To say it was weird would be an understatement. I should have thought to ask why I would need a special guide from an inner-earth dimension, but I didn't.

Over the years I've learned to accept that different guides will show up, depending on the work that I am doing. I have learned not to question why because I trust that at some point, I will figure it out. Sometimes I'm a little in awe that all of these different guides show up just to help me. No matter who they are, where they came from, or why they are there, I am grateful for each and every one of them.

My Dead Crew

Not long after my psychic reading, I had a freelance assignment to ghostwrite a book for a client, Annette. Annette works with angels for her energy healing practice. She calls on their assistance for a lot of different psychic needs.

One Sunday afternoon, Annette was going to clear a house and invited me to come along. It was a house she'd cleared before that belonged to her friend. She needed to go back again because the homeowners had recently reported some new paranormal activity: cupboards slamming on their own and a general feeling of being watched all the time.

It came up at the last minute, but my husband was already out somewhere with the kids, so I was free to go. As I got ready to leave, I felt a wave of excitement that I knew wasn't mine. My grandmothers were both there and announced they were coming along with me. When I got in the car, both Mac and Megan also showed up. I was confused.

My husband's best friend looked at me and said, "I'm coming with you. And you can tell Johnny that I've got your back."

I laughed. "I don't know if John wants to hear me explain that I'm talking to his dead best friend on a regular basis."

Mac just grinned.

I was surprised to see that Megan was with him, but I was glad to see her just the same.

I got in the car. "Buckle up," I said with a laugh. And I drove to a nearby suburb with a car full of dead people, still not entirely sure why they were all coming with me.

The house was a four-level split, probably from the late '80s or early '90s. Annette explained that one of the adult sons who lived with his parents was susceptible to attachments, and she assumed that's why we were back.

An attachment is when an intelligent energy attaches to a human energy. Sometimes, when people experience trauma, their auric fields become weak and susceptible to darker energies we can't see. Sometimes, we invite these darker energies in without even realizing it. Drinking excessively or using drugs can be all the opening a darker entity needs to jump in. Playing with a Ouija board is another way darker entities can gain access to our energy fields. Conducting a paranormal investigation without following certain protocols is yet another way our auric fields can become susceptible to foreign entities. In this case, I sensed that there were some mental health and addiction issues with one of the adult sons.

We walked in through the kitchen and went straight down to the basement to start.

"I tuned in before I came," Annette explained. "There's an energy line running through the neighborhood. I wouldn't be surprised if a lot of the houses in this neighborhood are haunted. I'm going to shift the energy to move up and over the house." She handed me a giant quartz crystal wand.

"Move this in a clockwise circle like this," she said, demonstrating. "I'm going to create a vortex of energy."

The homeowners watched and listened.

I closed my eyes and did what she asked. But I felt silly knowing the homeowners were watching. In my mind's eye, I could see a wall of energy growing on the outside of the house. It looked like a bike ramp that was getting bigger and bigger. The energy vortex grew into a tornado that swirled upward.

"Any ghosts moving along the energy line will now be able to see the vortex and use it like an elevator to get to heaven," she explained.

I concentrated on the wall of energy, but I didn't see any ghosts.

"There's one watching us from the hallway," she said. "He just stuck his tongue out at us."

As she said it, I could see him in my mind's eye. He was tall and rather skinny, wearing a dark gray jacket and what looked like jeans. He had longer, dark hair that looked like it needed a trim, glasses, and a mustache.

"I am going to go work with your son," Annette said to the homeowners.

"I'll take you upstairs," said her friend's husband.

"Just keep doing what you are doing," she said to me.

Great. Except... I didn't really know what I was doing.

"Have you been working with Annette very long?" her friend asked me.

"No," I said. "I'm helping her with her book and I just wanted to see what it was like to clear a house."

I closed my eyes, hoping that maybe this would end the small talk.

When I did, I could see the ghost guy in the hallway, watching me. He was taunting and teasing, and it was distracting. I always invoke an energy of protection in my work, and I wasn't afraid of him by any means. I imagine myself in a protective bubble. I ground myself to the earth's energy by imagining a cord connecting me to the earth. I stretch that cord up to the divine to keep me divinely guided in whatever it is I am doing. Within my bubble, I only allow light and love inside by specifically requesting that only those with my greatest and highest good in mind be allowed in my space.

But in this moment, I also added an energy of invisibility. I simply asked that only those souls with my greatest and highest good in mind be allowed to see or hear what I was doing. It worked instantly. I could see the perplexed look on his face, and I could feel his confusion not knowing or understanding where I'd gone. He wandered off down the hallway, probably to go see what Annette was up to.

"This is my first time doing anything like this. I'm not exactly sure what I'm supposed to do," I admitted.

I closed my eyes again and decided to practice. I tried to visualize the upstairs of the house. Having gone straight downstairs, I thought it would be a good test for my clairvoyant abilities. I tried to "see" the rooms upstairs in my mind's eye. That way, when I went upstairs, I could see how close I was to the real thing.

I could see the upstairs living room in my mind's eye, and I had a sense that there was an older, female ghost in this room.

"Do you know anything about the previous owners?" I asked Annette's friend.

"There was an elderly lady who passed away here," she said.

My gut told me that it was the same lady who was sitting upstairs in a rocking chair in the living room.

I could also see an office, the bedroom, and the bathroom. I sensed what I thought was the spirit of a teenage girl somewhere upstairs.

"Do you know anything about a teenage girl?" I asked.

"No, nothing," she said.

Annette called us both upstairs. Together, Annette and I went about clearing the house with Florida Water and sage spray. (Normally, I prefer to burn sage and palo santo, but in this case, the homeowner was especially sensitive to smoke.) Annette also uses a singing bowl to determine when the energy is clear. She waits for the bowl to make the perfect tone and that's how she knows when she is done.

"Did you pick up on anything in the house?" Annette asked.

I told her about the lady in the living room. She agreed, and then she sat down on the couch. After a few moments, I realized she was whispering to someone ... and figured out that she was talking to the elderly ghost.

As she sat there whispering, I got a download of information. I knew that this lady was the former owner. I knew that she really liked the family that had moved in after she'd died. She felt protective and watchful over them, especially because of the energy line in the neighborhood. She knew that the area was a highway of sorts, and she worried about the family. I repeated everything out loud for the sake of the homeowners who were listening. Annette agreed with everything I said. Next she called in the angels to do a sweep of the room and, with my eyes closed, I could see them moving through the room: north and south, east and west. In my image, they were holding push brooms and they were very efficient.

I felt a pat on my arm. Surprised, I opened my eyes and said out loud, "I just felt someone pat my arm."

"The old lady gave you a pat on the arm as she walked by," said Annette.

And that's exactly what it felt like, the sort of pat an elderly person gives when they are saying thank you for something. I could feel her gratitude.

After we had finished all of the other rooms, Annette asked the homeowners to walk through every room in the house to see if anything still felt off.

"Did you feel any sort of younger presence?" I asked while we were waiting. "Maybe that of a teenage girl? When I scanned the house from downstairs, I felt something that felt like the presence of a younger ghost."

Annette thought about it for a minute. "No," she said. "I don't get anything like that."

I screwed my face up in concentration. I could have sworn there was the energy of a teenage girl.

Annette thought for a minute. "You know, we created the energy vortex when we were downstairs. Maybe you sensed someone who felt called to it and passed by on their way to heaven?"

That made sense to me, but that's not what it felt like. But then again, who was I to argue? This was the first time I had ever attempted to do anything like this.

One of the homeowners returned. "The office still feels off," she said. "It feels a bit muggy in there."

We all went to check it out. As we walked through the door, Annette gave a startled cry.

"What?" asked the homeowner.

"There's your teenage girl," she said to me, pointing to the chair opposite the desk.

As soon as she said the words, I closed my eyes and I could "see" a girl in my mind's eye. She was sitting sideways in one of the chairs opposite the desk. Her legs were crossed and looped over the arm of the chair and she was swinging them—up and down, up and down. She looked like she was about sixteen or seventeen years old. She was blond, and she looked filthy. The little bit of the download that came with her suggested that she'd been a runaway. Whatever the case, she had a whole lot of attitude. She glared at me with a look in her eyes that said loud and clear, "You can't make me do anything I don't want to do."

Annette asked the homeowner where she'd gotten the chairs. She reported that she'd just bought them a few months ago from someone on Craigslist.

At this point, I had nearly forgotten that I had come to the house with my own entourage. But behind me, Megan spoke up. "I'm here for her. She's the reason I came."

I was surprised. Up to that point, the crew I had brought along had mostly stayed in the background.

"She doesn't want to cross for the same reason I didn't want to cross," said Megan.

I took a deep breath.

Out loud and keeping my eyes closed, I explained that my friend Megan was the first soul I had ever helped find her way to heaven, and that she had come along with me.

"The reason she came," I explained, "was specifically to help this girl. This girl doesn't want to go to heaven for the same reasons Megan didn't want to go to heaven."

Surprised, the dead girl looked up at me and stopped swinging her legs.

"Megan didn't want to go to heaven because she was worried she would have to see someone she didn't want to see," I explained to everyone in the room, including the dead girl.

I turned my attention just to her. "Megan is here to reassure you that you don't have to see anyone you don't want to see." I knew Megan wanted to be there to help this girl in the same way Mac had helped Megan.

The ghost girl was surprised. Without a word or hesitation, she got up out of her chair and went with Megan.

Driving home, I used the time to process everything that had just happened. My first house clearing had been a success. I was grateful to have had an entire entourage with me.

Only Mac was left in the car with me. He told me again that he would be there whenever I needed him, and he said he "always had my back."

I hadn't known Mac very well in life. We'd gone to the same high school, and he had been my husband's best friend. But I hadn't dated my husband in high school. A shy, introverted wallflower, I had probably barely even talked to either one of them back then. But after we started dating, I had heard story after story about Mac. To have him sitting with me now, offering to help me, was overwhelming.

I was overwhelmed with gratitude that he would be there for me if I ever needed him. I was also overwhelmed (again) by how incredible it was to say that I knew someone better in death than I ever had in life.

I tried to figure out how I could possibly explain to my husband what had happened. When he asked me how my afternoon had gone, I simply answered, "Fine."

I could barely wrap my own head around everything that had just happened to me, and I was still trying to make sense of whatever these gifts were and what I was supposed to be doing with them. I had no idea how I was going to be able to explain any of this to anyone else.

It has taken a while, but over time, I've been able to begin to explain to others what it is that I do.

With ghost energies, I see them as stuck in an in-between dimension, something between this earthly plane and what I think of as heaven. They are operating at a low vibration and often, for me, they "feel" heavier. A spirit energy is different. A spirit is the energy (or soul) of someone who has gone to where they were supposed to when they died, but they've come back to visit loved ones still here on Earth. Once a ghost crosses over to where they are supposed to be, they reach a higher vibration and have more clarity. Their energy is transcendent and they can come back to visit their loved ones on the earthly plane whenever they want. Because they are operating at a higher vibration, they can actually be of assistance to those they want to help.

In this case, my Mafia guide, Mac and Megan, and my grandmothers were operating at a high vibration. The runaway ghost girl was at a heavier, lower vibration. It was one of the first times I began to distinguish between the different types of energy.

The Palmer House Hotel

The Palmer House Hotel in Sauk Centre, Minnesota, has been named the "best haunted hotel in America" by *USA Today*.[2] It has been investigated by Zak Bagans and featured on television shows like *Ghost Adventures*[3] and more recently by *The Dead Files*.[4]

But even more important than all of that, the Palmer House has become my home away from home. It's the only hotel where I feel like I can walk through the lobby in my socks and not even think twice about it. The staff and owners are my extended adopted family that came into my life at exactly the right time. They are the family I got to choose.

Every time I go to this historic haunted hotel, without fail, I learn something new about my gifts, my abilities, and myself. I've attended classes there, I've taught classes there, and I go any chance I get. The "unregistered guests" (i.e., ghosts and spirits)

. . . .

2. "Palmer House Hotel Wins Best Haunted Hotel," USA Today, accessed March 4, 2020, https://www.10best.com/awards/travel/best-haunted-hotel-2015/.

3. "Ghost Adventures Films at The Palmer House Hotel," Palmer House, accessed March 4, 2020, http://www.thepalmerhousehotel.com/ghost-adventures-filming/.

4. James Wray, "The Dead Files Asks: Is the Palmer House Hotel Haunted?", IMDb, February 24, 2018, https://www.imdb.com/news/ni61933462.

have taught me an infinite number of lessons about my psychic gifts and how they work. The Palmer House has taught me that buildings have souls, and its soul is complicated, intricate, and beautiful.

The first time I stayed at the Palmer House, I was still far from calling myself "psychic." I was there with my Ghost Stories Ink group and we were hosting an event. Our agenda included writing and art classes and featured a paranormal investigation. The first morning, I was startled awake because I felt like something was watching me. Lying there with my eyes closed, I was afraid to open them. I wasn't sure if I was ready to see who was standing there. If I had to guess, I would have guessed a little boy. I had finally convinced myself it was just my imagination and was about to open my eyes when I felt someone reach over to hold my hand. Still, I somehow managed to convince myself it was just my overactive imagination. But now, I know better.

I have since learned to lock in my space when I stay there. I am happy to hang out and talk to the ghosts at the Palmer House, but I don't need them standing over me, watching me sleep. I lock in my space in the same way I do when I put up a protective shield or bubble. I ask that only those souls or energies with my greatest and highest good be allowed inside, and then I ask my guides to guard my space and keep it safe. When I stay in a hotel room at the Palmer House, I simply extend this protective bubble to include my whole room. I often feel like my guides even stand guard at the door. In fact, at one of our events, a guest took a photo in the middle of the night of a tall, dark figure standing outside one of the doors in the hallway. When I saw the post on social media, I realized the dark shadow was standing right outside my room. I knew instantly it was a protective presence, but it took me a while (and a series of pendulum questions) to realize that it was Mac.

One of my favorite rooms at the Palmer House Hotel is room 17, which is also known as Lucy's room. Lucy was a "lady of the night" back in a time when people, especially women, didn't have a lot of options. The first time I stayed in her room with Jessica, I was already more comfortable with my new label, "psychic." I could feel Lucy watching us when we came in, trying to assess who we were and what we were doing. We were careful to keep our room neat (Lucy doesn't like messes). We also left her chair for her and made a point not to sit in it. After the first night, I could feel her staring at me in the corner, as if she were trying to figure us out. The next night, we were getting ready for our event and we were both doing our hair and putting on makeup. I felt an overwhelming sadness from her in the corner. She wanted to go out and have a fun girls' night too.

We both told her that we loved staying in her room because it felt like we were staying with a girlfriend. We told her she was our girlfriend and we always enjoyed our time with her when we stayed in her room. The next morning, I woke up and she wasn't staring at us from across the room ... she was lying right in between both of us in the giant king-size bed.

Now, when I stay in her room, I really do feel like I am staying with a girlfriend (except ... she is dead). Even though I typically lock in my space, I always allow Lucy to stay in there with me if she wants. I don't feel right blocking her out of what has become her own room. I trust her not to mess with me.

One time, I was staying at the hotel to help out with an event and conduct tours. There was a group of men staying in her room. It was a busy day and I was running around, helping anyone and everyone who needed it—in the bar, serving food, or even helping to turn over a room here or there.

I was walking up the main staircase and suddenly, Lucy was right there next to me to complain about the people staying in her room.

"I can't do anything about that," I said. "They are paying to stay there. But if you don't like them, you are always welcome to come stay with me if you need to."

She stomped off in a huff and didn't talk to me for a while after that.

Over time, I've come to realize that there are a lot of ghosts at the Palmer House who have chosen to stay behind in order to help us learn more about the other side. Some of these ghosts are even helpful. There is a ghost in the kitchen who is very protective of the Palmer House and its staff. When something is wrong in the kitchen, she pushes the mixing bowls off the top of the freezer to let everyone know.

Mrs. Palmer herself comes back often to check on the Palmer House. Mrs. Palmer is operating at a high vibration. She has crossed over and is choosing to come back to help out in this realm. It's almost as if Kelley Freese is the owner and manages the living staff on this side of the veil, and Mrs. Palmer manages the unregistered guests and staff on the other side of the veil.

TWO
YOU WANT TO GO
TO HEAVEN *HOW?*

One of the most comforting things I have learned with this gift is that heaven isn't as nearly as far away as we might think. Sometimes the souls I see, like my grandmothers, are here to visit us, offer us guidance, or offer their help. Part of their heaven is choosing to come back and check on us.

I was raised Catholic. My kids have gone to Catholic schools. I've made peace with the work that I do and what my faith sometimes teaches about the work that I do. Part of the Golden Rule instructs us to "Love thy neighbor as thyself." I like to add, "Even if your neighbor happens to be a ghost."

When I was trying to figure out what to do with these "gifts" I actually spent a lot of time in church. I would often go to morning Mass after I dropped the kids off at school. This was my favorite because it was quiet and quick. But mostly, I appreciated it because it wasn't a Mass of "obligation," which made the collective energy fantastic. Everyone in the church was there because they wanted to be there, which isn't always the case on Sundays.

When I'm at church, I like looking around to see who else has loved ones with them that they might not realize are there. My grandmothers (both deceased at the time) would come with me. I don't think they liked each other very much when they were alive because they always have me sit in the middle. I would sit there and, most days, ask some variation of the question, "Are you sure this is what I am supposed to be doing with my gifts?" And the answer would often come in the form of a song that would pop into my head. It was a song that had been a favorite church song of mine from my childhood, "Be Not Afraid."

But as far as religion goes, the Catholic faith does have an element of mysticism. There is a lot of talk about the Holy Spirit and all of the angels and saints. This isn't just talk. Our loved ones aren't the only ones who show up for Mass.

Not long ago, my oldest son, Avery, went through the sacrament of confirmation. Confirmation is my favorite of the sacraments. After all, it features the Holy Spirit. During my own confirmation, when I was an eighth grader, I remember feeling the energy of the Holy Spirit and being keenly aware that something else was there—a "holy" energy, so to speak.

Two days before my son's actual confirmation at the cathedral, his school (and our church) held a celebratory evening Mass for family members. There were two spaces reserved near the front, behind my eighth grader. The rest of the family had to sit in back. My brother (Avery's sponsor) and I started moving toward the front to sit by my son. I felt my grandmother's confusion. She wasn't sure if she should sit with me or my mom (her daughter).

And then she remembered.

"Oh, that's right," I heard her say in my ear as though she were talking to herself. "I don't have to choose because I don't have a body. I can sit with both of you." And she did.

During the Mass, the service included an incantation to the saints, naming them one at a time to call them in. Slowly, the room began to feel crowded—even more crowded than the families filling the pews to be with their eighth graders. I realized the saints were filling the room as their names were called. They stood in the aisles and around the room. They were everywhere.

It was a little overwhelming—and incredibly humbling—to feel their presence and know they were there. I wanted to hit my brother and say, "Hey. There's Saint John the Baptist in the corner next to Saint Elizabeth." But I didn't. I am pretty sure he wouldn't have believed me anyway.

———

Another time, I had an unexpected passenger drop by while I was on my way to the Palmer House to help out with an event. Exactly a two-hour drive from St. Paul, my car practically knows its way all on its own. I always use this time to pull myself together, especially if I am by myself. I let go of anything that held me in at home—the kids' stuff, work assignments, and other stressors. I look forward to having time to myself to work on my writing. I also tune in to the hotel to "check in" with the energy.

About an hour from Sauk Centre, an extra passenger jumped into the car with me. From the middle of the back seat, I felt a presence. It was a high-vibration energy. I sensed immediately that the spirit with me was Isaiah, Cara's son. Cara is the bar manager at the Palmer House. Isaiah had passed unexpectedly after an illness a few years before. I knew that he liked to pop by and say hello to his mom while she was at work, but I had no idea why he would show up in my car to talk to me.

He seemed really excited that I was going to the Palmer House, which was a little confusing for me because I'd never had an interaction with him before this. He specifically wanted me to ask his mom if "she liked the song." This made no sense to me, but I told him I would do my best. He also wanted me to tell her that he was always around to protect her if she ever needed it. Knowing Cara, she probably already knew that.

As I exited the highway and drove into Sauk Centre, I wondered about my interaction with Isaiah. I asked for some validation that this really happened. I suggested that if it was really Isaiah, then it would be helpful if Cara was the first person I saw when I got to the Palmer House. Two minutes later, I pulled into the parking lot and saw Cara standing on the back step outside the kitchen by herself, smoking a cigarette.

Seeing her standing there left me a little in awe. I hadn't known if she would be working that day. The fact that she was standing there by herself, after I had just asked for that, sent shivers down to my toes.

I told her about my extra passenger. I asked her about the song and passed along Isaiah's cryptic message. She instantly knew what it was about. Through her tears, Cara explained that the night before, a specific song had played on the radio, just as she'd been thinking about something. Then she asked if Isaiah had been changing the radio station in the bar. For the last week, the radio in the bar kept inexplicably changing itself to the "I Love the '90s" channel. Often, it happened to be when the song "O.P.P." was blaring, and it would blare through the dining room. She'd tried to figure out if someone had been changing the channel, but the only other person around was another waitress who didn't even know how to work the remote.

I have a lot of natural protection around me when I am going about my day. I think my guides and angels do a good job of making sure that I don't get interrupted all day long. When Isaiah showed up with a message for his mom, it was unusual and unexpected. Through this, I learned that if my guides do let someone come through while I am going about my day, it's important.

Stairway to Heaven

One summer night, my Ghost Stories Ink group was invited to be the nightly entertainment for an alumni gathering. They wanted us to lead them on a ghost hunt of the supposedly haunted Hamline University in St. Paul. We knew it would be very different than any of our other events. Usually, guests who sign up for our events are already interested in the paranormal and have a basic understanding of who we are and what we do. We expect a few skeptics, or less-than-enthusiastic participants, because every now and then a guest will bring a significant other who might not be that excited about participating. But with this event, where so many attendees were just "along for the ride," we knew there might be more disinterested and unenthusiastic people on our ghost hunt than usual. We wanted to make sure we were as prepared as possible.

As part of our preparation, Jessica and I went on a tour the week before to get a feel for the campus and try to determine the best places to conduct a paranormal investigation. We followed our university contact around, in and out of various buildings, and listened as he told stories about the school.

After, we sat by ourselves at an outdoor table just outside one of the buildings. Coincidentally, it was right in front of the building where I'd spent three years in law school. Our table was practically on top of the exact spot where I had graduated from Hamline University School of Law. The significance was not lost on me.

We talked about different impressions that we'd gotten in different buildings. We both noted that when we walked into one of the residence halls, there was a dark, heavy wave of really depressing energy that was overpowering the lobby. Neither of us wanted to mention it in front of our tour guide. We agreed that someone (we both thought a young man) had probably committed suicide in that hall at some point, if not that exact space.

But we also agreed that once we walked through the front hall and back into the community area, the darkness lifted a bit.

Normally, we would have been all about investigating the dark, creepy, heavy corners. But this was a group of writers, not necessarily paranormal enthusiasts. We thought it would be better to conduct our investigation in the lighter community area.

The night of our investigation arrived and we eventually found ourselves sitting in that community room. As we sat there, explaining our equipment and answering questions about ghosts, we told the story of how heavy and dark the front entrance of the building felt when we first walked through. I could sense a curiosity, and I felt the darkness coming into the room.

During an investigation, it can sometimes feel a little silly to be talking to the air, asking questions to someone you can't see. I was especially self-conscious about it on this night. Our attendees were curious about what we were doing, but a lot of our attendees were only vaguely interested in the paranormal. However, Jessica always brings a seriousness and kindness to our investigations that makes everyone in the group (both living and dead) feel at ease.

Sitting there in the residence hall at Hamline University, it felt like whoever was there was listening to our every word. I started to speak.

"I'm feeling a curious presence," I said to everyone.

That dark presence had come in to hear what we had to say. While it wasn't interested in interacting with our equipment, it wanted to hear what we had to say about death and dying. We started to talk about heaven and how, no matter what, everyone deserved to go. Ghosts didn't have to stay stuck in an earthbound afterlife if they didn't want to.

Nothing happened. There wasn't a swirl of energy; nothing knocked on the wall in agreement or anything, and the conversation moved on to other topics. The night wrapped up shortly after that and nothing more came of it... until two nights later.

I woke up suddenly at 3:00 a.m. (This was the point where I began to sense a theme. If I get woken up at 3:00 a.m., it usually means I'm on call and have to help someone... or something.) And there, in my mind's eye, in my bedroom at 3:00 a.m., was a young college kid. He was a hippie of sorts, right out of the late '60s or early '70s. His hair was dark and shaggy and his clothes were uber cool. He was wearing a jacket I could have seen on the mannequin at my favorite vintage shop. I knew right away, without being able to explain how I knew, that he was the same boy from the Hamline University residence hall.

He looked at me and said, "Can I have a stairway to heaven like the song?"

It took me a few minutes to find my words.

"You can go to heaven however you want," I finally answered.

And just like that, a stairway dropped out of the sky and he started walking up. The song "Stairway to Heaven" by Led Zeppelin played in the background. It's a really long song, so it was a really long staircase. I watched him walk up, taking each step one at a time until he was gone.

After, I lay awake for a long time. It was the first time a complete stranger had showed up needing my help. It wouldn't be the last.

Your Bus Will Be Here Any Minute

One Fourth of July weekend, we had visitors from abroad. Our good friends (they are British) were touring around the United States, having flown in from Gibraltar for their summer holiday. They fit a stop to see us in their itinerary and wanted to experience a Minnesota weekend at the lake.

We rented a condo unit at Ruttger's Lodge, just north of Mille Lacs Lake. Our family had a downstairs unit with a full kitchen while our friends took the unit above. We let the kids sleep in the bedroom, and my husband and I slept on the pull-out sofa.

One night at 3:00 a.m. we were startled awake by a loud crash in the kitchen. With a rush of adrenaline, my husband and I flew out of bed to see what happened. We found the toaster in the middle of the kitchen floor. It had fallen off its perch on top of the refrigerator. Although, standing there staring at it in the middle of the kitchen, I got a strong sense that it had been pushed to get my attention.

Tuning in to my guide, I got an image in my head of a school bus. My Mafia spirit guide was standing just outside the door of it, holding a clipboard and reading off names from a list. As he read each name, a different person would step forward to get on the bus. One of the people getting on the bus turned to me and said, "It isn't very often that someone like you comes to this area. We've been waiting for this bus for a while."

The last person climbed on the bus and the bus drove off to heaven. I didn't even have to do anything. This experience taught me that whenever I have a whole crowd of people who need help, a bus is an efficient method to get them all where they need to go.

When my oldest son completed his confirmation, it was at the Cathedral of St. Paul. The cathedral has a darker energy than most churches I've been in. It's heavy. My middle son has since toured the cathedral with his class and mentioned that there is a stone from the castle where Joan of Arc was imprisoned, which could be a reason it feels intense. But most likely, it's a lot of things that all add up. In any event, I usually stay on high alert when I'm there, and I wasn't at all disappointed when we realized the pew reserved for our family was in one of the last rows, the farthest away from the altar and right next to the exit.

It was a weeknight, and the service was long. We didn't see much of it from the back of the church, but because I was still impressed by the presence of the saints a few days prior, I was fine with it. I felt like we'd already had our saintly experience; this was just a formality.

Later that night, after everyone was home and tucked in, I was startled awake in the middle of the night. There were a lot of lost souls at the cathedral who needed help—there are a lot of Catholics who put themselves in purgatory because they don't think they are good enough to go to heaven. In my mind's eye, a bus pulled up to the front doors of the cathedral. Several Catholics from all different time periods came out the same doors I'd been sitting near and walked down the steps to the street. An older priest came out separately.

As soon as everyone else saw the priest, they recoiled in fear. But I knew he was supposed to get on the bus. Except...no one else would get on the bus if the priest was going too. I had to figure out how to let him get on the bus without anyone else knowing he was there. I decided that the priest should go last. After everyone else was settled, but before he got on, I wrapped him up in a big bubble of invisibility. No one else even noticed he was there and everyone drove off together to heaven.

Going to Heaven on a Harley

One winter day I got a phone call from Kelley, the owner of the Palmer House Hotel. It was the first time a set of stainless-steel mixing bowls had gone flying off the top of the freezer rather dramatically. The crash and clang they made when they smashed to the ground nearly gave anyone within earshot a heart attack.

But also, two waitresses who never see anything paranormal had both reported seeing a dark shadow pacing back and forth in front of the stove. She was wondering if I could tune in and see what was going on.

The first thing that came to mind when she told me about the mixing bowls was the incident over the Fourth of July weekend when the toaster got thrown off the top of the fridge. It seemed to have the same energy—a spirit wanting to get someone's attention.

I found a quiet moment in my day to check in. I'd done remote work before, but not necessarily like this. This time, I'd be trying to tune in to a specific situation and discern what was going on. My guides (and my third eye) didn't seem too concerned about not being in the same physical location, because my sixth sense immediately told me that these were two separate incidents.

The mixing bowls getting thrown off the top of the freezer was actually one of the regular kitchen ghosts who wanted to make sure she got Kelley's attention. It had to be something strong enough to make sure Kelley took it seriously and paid attention. But she certainly wasn't trying to hurt anyone.

I've since gotten to know this ghost rather well. I'm not the greatest with names, but I believe hers is Sarah, and she is very protective of Kelley and the Palmer House. Whenever she thinks something is wrong, she pushes the mixing bowls off the top of the freezer. When it happens now, Kelley knows to check in with someone about it. It's a creative way to communicate, but it seems to be working.

In this case, the "something wrong" Sarah was trying to draw attention to was a dark shadow figure pacing back and forth, back and forth in front of the stove just inside the back door.

I got a download of information and it was a whole story all at once. He was a young man in his late twenties or early thirties. He was really angry that he was dead. He had died in some sort of an ATV accident, most likely a snowmobile, and my sense was that it was alcohol related. I thought his name started with an S: maybe Shawn? Or Stephen? But again, I'm not that great at getting names.

He was really, really mad that he had done something so stupid as to get himself killed. His girlfriend (or maybe fiancée or new wife) was pregnant with (or had just recently had) their baby girl. Maybe she was pregnant when he died and by now she'd had the baby?

The download of information also told me that he was from the area. When he died, it was so sudden and he was so angry about it that he missed his window of white light. Now he was stuck and wasn't sure what to do or where to go. He knew that the Palmer House was haunted, and there was some sort of an indirect connection to the hotel—it's possible he was a friend of a friend who had worked there (past or present). But now that he'd found his way to the Palmer House through the back loading dock door, he was afraid to go past the kitchen—because he was afraid of ghosts. Which wasn't ironic at all. (Insert eye roll here.)

He was so angry he didn't really want to listen to me, but he also didn't know what else to do. I was fascinated that even though I wasn't really "there" in the kitchen of the Palmer House, he could still see, sense, and hear me.

I explained, "You can't stay at the Palmer House."

I knew he could hear me and was listening to me, but he didn't stop pacing.

"If you cross over and go to heaven, you'll be able to come back and be with her and the baby."

He stopped for a split second, like he was confused about how I knew, but then he went back to pacing.

"How are you supposed to help anyone by pacing back and forth in the kitchen of the Palmer House? Are you planning to do that for all eternity?"

He stopped and looked at me as if he were seeing me for the first time.

In that moment, I realized I was talking to him as if I were a lawyer cross-examining a witness in court. I use the same tactic with my children when I want to talk them into doing something. I couldn't help but laugh ... here I was, using my legal training and questioning expertise to persuade a ghost to go where he was supposed to go. I filed that under "ways I never expected to use my law degree." But I wouldn't be adding that to the alumni update any time soon.

"You can go to heaven however you want," I said, deliberately changing the subject. "I had one guy who wanted to go to heaven on a stairway like the song. Do you want a stairway to heaven like the song?"

"That's dumb," he told me. "Why would I want to do that?"

And in that moment, I knew two things. The stairway to heaven was real. It wasn't something I made up. I also knew that this moment was real too. If I'd been making either of these two situations up, it would have worked the exact same way both times upon my suggestion. Finally, after this, I was able to stop questioning my gift and the psychic information coming in. I was finally learning to trust that this was how it worked for me and my guides weren't going to lead me down the wrong path.

"Do you want to go to heaven on a snowmobile?" I figured if he'd died snowmobiling, maybe he'd want to take one to heaven?

Instead, I got an image in my head of a really beautiful Harley-Davidson motorcycle.

"You want to go to heaven on a Harley?" I asked.

He smiled.

"Okay, that's cool. But you actually have to go to heaven, you can't just drive it around." I thought for a minute and added, "And when you get there, you can keep it. And just in case, I'm sending my friend Mac along with you to make sure you don't get lost or distracted."

He seemed okay with all of that because he left the Palmer House kitchen and went out the back door. There, next to the dumpster in the parking lot, was the Harley motorcycle for him, and next to him was my friend Mac on his own motorcycle. The guy climbed on his new Harley and together they rode away.

I called Kelley and told her the whole story. She went back into the kitchen and reported back that everything felt light and fresh—definitely a different energy than before.

Over time, I have learned that different souls might need to see and hear different things to help them move on. It turns out there are a lot of ways to get to heaven.

THREE
MISCONCEPTIONS
ABOUT HEAVEN

I learned about purgatory at my Catholic grade school. Purgatory was for those souls who weren't good enough to go to heaven. They weren't bad enough to go to hell, but they were destined to spend eternity in a place that I imagined was somewhere between heaven and earth. A lot of my work has been to help some of the souls who put themselves in a purgatory of sorts because they don't believe they are good enough to go to heaven.

Life on Earth is hard. We are here to make mistakes and learn lessons. Just because we may not have learned a lesson in exactly the right way doesn't mean that we aren't allowed to go where we are supposed to go. In my work, sometimes souls need to be convinced that they are good enough to go to what they believe is heaven.

One of my first encounters with a soul who was stuck for this reason was one of my very own ancestors. As I ventured further along my psychic path, part of my process was to seek out other healers and mentors. During one of these sessions with a mentor, someone from my mother's side of the family showed up—he was a ghost who needed some help.

This member of my family from long ago had some issues. My mom remembers a story that was whispered when she was young about how the family had to move from one state to another far away because "there'd been some trouble."

During my session, we looked back at my ancestors and one stepped forward. As we talked about my mother's side of the family, I suddenly became filled with fear. Together, my mentor and I deduced that I had experience with him in a past life.

The more I do this work, the more I see and know that our soul is multifaceted beyond what we can easily understand. I have seen enough evidence in my work to believe in past lives.

As the story began to drop in, I realized it was more than just that I'd known him in a past life—I had been married to him.

I felt like I needed to cover my head with my hands; it felt like I was cowering in a corner. I had been married to him, but I had been very afraid of his quick temper and seething anger.

Suddenly, the perspective shifted. An overwhelming feeling of guilt came over me and I got a story download. He was still stuck in this world because he didn't think he was good enough to go to heaven. Something bad had happened in his lifetime and he felt terrible about it. He put himself into an eternity of purgatory in order to "make it right" for his ancestors to follow. He'd been sticking around my family for a long time trying to "help."

But that creates a problem. When a soul is trying to help from the in-between dimension, they are functioning at a much lower vibration of energy. They aren't really able to help and assist us at all. More often than not, they just get in the way and hold us back. In order for our loved ones to help those they love still on Earth, they need to cross over first, where they will reach a higher energetic vibration. Then, they can come back and help us out and be much more effective.

Even after explaining all of this, my ancestor still didn't think he was worthy to go to heaven. Together we explained that heaven was a loving place filled with forgiveness. But he still didn't seem ready. At this point, it seemed like he needed to tell someone his story before he could find peace.

I asked him to tell me what he'd done, especially if that would help him in some way. Almost immediately, my ribs began to hurt. I knew, without a doubt, that he had killed someone, either by stabbing or shooting them in the chest. I was feeling the pain not because I was the one he had killed, but because that was his way to communicate to me what had happened.

I explained what was going on out loud. I also said, "It must have been really hard to be an early American pioneer, coming to a new land and living every day with so much fear. When those pioneers arrived in what was then a New World, with so much work to do just to live each day, they probably wanted to turn right around and go home again. But logistics didn't exactly make that possible."

My friend explained, "Your crime was committed a long, long time ago. There is no one left on Earth who remembers your mistake."

"If you go on to the light," I added, "you will be able to come back. You will be able to come back and help whatever family members you wish to assist."

And that's how he would have a better opportunity to make it right.

I could sense him finally giving in and going. About an hour later, out of nowhere, I felt an overwhelming sense of gratitude and I knew it was him. I was just glad his soul had finally found peace. No one deserves to suffer overwhelming, crippling guilt for something that happened over a hundred years ago.

———————

Later that night, I remembered being in junior high. There was a stretch of time in seventh grade where I had been terrified to go to sleep alone in my room. There was often a dark shadow in the corner. I insisted someone was watching me sleep. Everyone else I trusted enough to tell about it insisted that there was no such thing as ghosts and that I had an overactive imagination. But now, looking back, I know it was probably him.

I can't go back to those nights when I'd been so afraid, but I am grateful to be at a place where I can now better understand who and what it was.

Everyone Is "Good Enough" for Heaven

Recently, we were at the Cathedral of St. Paul again for Easter Sunday Mass. Our seats were near the front. During one of the readings, I felt a group of lost souls moving in from the back and crowding around the outside aisles. It was Easter Sunday after all—it felt like they were coming into church to see if they were finally good enough to go to heaven.

In my experience, everyone is good enough to go to heaven. With all of the souls I've helped, I've never once had someone hear, "Nope, I'm sorry, you can't come in. You're not good enough." We are all good enough.

I started working with one of my guides to open up a tunnel of light in the pillar near the altar. By the time we got to the homily, Archangel Michael had appeared at the entrance to the tunnel. One by one, each lost soul stepped forward as if in a procession and walked into the light and through the tunnel.

I guess I know where I will be spending Easter Sunday from now on. Going to Mass for Easter has never felt so important.

Heaven Is Whatever You Want It to Be

It didn't take me long to realize that if I was doing this kind of energy clearing and protection work at some of the state's most notoriously haunted properties, maybe I should be helping homeowners too. It had become a calling I couldn't ignore.

Through my work I was getting better at identifying the two types of energies that can haunt a home: residual energy and intelligent energy.

An intelligent haunting is when a ghost is interacting with people in a space. For example, an intelligent haunting can be knocks on a wall in response to a question. Furniture or items can be moved around by an unseen hand. Disembodied voices can even try to talk and communicate. Intelligent energy is an actual ghost or a spirit, something that is trying to intelligently communicate. This energy can be cleared, but usually it involves a conversation with the ghost to convince them that they need to move on to where they are supposed to go. Again, this is because all souls have freewill choice in death as they do in life.

A residual haunting is energy that is emitted and trapped in a space, almost like a recording. For example, when the same thing happens at the same time every night for twenty years, that energy can leave an imprint. Footsteps walking down the hall at the same time every night can be residual energy. Or if something tragic happened in a space—like a murder—an energy imprint of that tragic moment can be left behind. For example, if a scream is heard at the same time every night, that can be residual energy. Residual energy can be cleared and metaphysical practitioners use a variety of tools, methods, and practices to clear residual energy.

A client hired me to come clear her house. She had been seeing a ghost of a man in her house. This ghost had realized she could see him and he was having a lot of fun startling her.

I decided to invite my mother to come with for this clearing. We have taken a few psychic development classes together, and she has a master's degree in holistic health. She does a great job of explaining some of the science behind energy and I knew she would be able to explain everything really well to my client.

We both tuned in to our client's house a few days before we were scheduled to go there. I usually try to scan the house I am going to clear in advance. If there is a lost soul I can usually help them before I even go to the property, and then it gives the house two or three days to settle before I go to clear it. In this case, I picked up on an old man.

His story download followed immediately. He had never lived in the house, but he was from the neighborhood. He had always liked the gardens at this particular house, and perhaps had even worked there at one time as a gardener. When his ghostly self figured out that the homeowner could see him, he decided to have a little fun. He was bored and scaring her not only gave him an energy boost, it gave him a purpose. This felt like a bad combination for a ghost: to be bored and intention-ally mischievous.

His download also told me that his wife had preceded him in death. He didn't like his wife very much when she was alive. When he passed away (from what felt to me like a heart attack), his wife showed up to take him to heaven. He looked at her, said, "No thanks," and decided to stay right where he was. He didn't want to go anywhere if she was going to be there too.

"Heaven isn't what you think it is," I told him.

He turned to look at me. I could see what he thought heaven was. It included a lot of singing, standing in quiet rows, and prayerful reverence ... and his wife.

"It doesn't have to be like that."

I could tell he was listening to me.

"First of all, you don't have to see anyone you don't want to see. If you don't ever want to see your wife again, you don't have to."

He didn't respond, but I could still feel him listening.

"I can see you stay here because you like the gardens."

He nodded.

"Did you know that when you go to heaven, if all you want to do is garden every minute of every day, that is perfectly acceptable? You can garden all day if you want."

I could feel his excitement. He was ready to go.

For some reason, my guides showed me an elevator. I got the sense that maybe he was fascinated by elevators. So out in front of the homeowner's property, I visualized an elevator that went to heaven. He got in and left. I decided to leave it there, just in case there were any others in the neighborhood that might be looking for some way to get to heaven. One of my guides set it up so that it was a one-way transport to heaven. Souls who were stuck in between this world and the next would be drawn to it, for reasons they might not even understand. Once inside, they would feel the clarity and peace they would need to take it to where they were supposed to go.

―――――――

Two days later, we sat in the homeowner's living room, telling our client about the gardener and explaining why he hadn't wanted to go to heaven. My mom had picked up on an older woman who also needed our help to cross, making me glad I had invited her to come with.

This woman wasn't haunting the house, but she was somehow connected to the homeowner. It seemed almost like she showed up because there was an opportunity and she didn't want to miss it. It felt like perhaps she was an ancestor or relative of some sort. In any event, she felt very ready to get to wherever she needed to go.

She looked thin and prim and proper. Her lips were pursed together and as we talked about the gardener ghost, I could feel her impatience. She was trying to be patient and wait her turn while we talked about him, but really she just wanted us to hurry up so she could be on her way too.

We started talking about her and what we could do to help.

For some reason, I wasn't really getting much—if any—information about her like I usually did. There wasn't any sort of story download like I usually get and that was a little confusing. In this case, I used that as confirmation that I wasn't making it up. If I were making it up, my imagination would have come up with some sort of dramatic story for her.

Maybe it was because she was already ready to go and she didn't need to be convinced. She didn't need us to tell her story, she just needed a way to get to the light.

But the problem was, I also didn't have any information about how to get her to go or how to help her cross. I wasn't coming up with much of anything about what she wanted or needed, so in my mind's eye, I just decided to call in a bubble of light.

From across the room, my mom got excited. "Oh!" she said. "She just got really excited and asked me if it was like the bubble from *The Wizard of Oz* that takes Glinda the Good Witch wherever she wants to go?"

"I guess that's exactly what it is," I said, happy that we'd found what she needed. I didn't think I knew what she wanted to see, but my guides still showed me exactly what would work for her. This situation helped me to realize that sometimes, I just need to get out of my own way.

After this, the homeowner reported that everything seemed lighter and more clear. Her house felt much better. I was especially glad that the old gardener was able to find an afterlife that agreed with him.

Heaven Isn't Boring

In my work, I've learned that I'm never really on vacation, especially when I think I'm on vacation. Not long ago, we took our kids to Florida for the first time to enjoy a family vacation over their spring break. We have become big fans of sites like Vrbo and Airbnb as a way to find vacation lodging for a family of five. It never once occurred to me that these houses could potentially be haunted. We found (what we thought was) an amazing house on Marco Island, three blocks from the public beach access.

We arrived and settled in. A few nights into our stay, I woke up in the middle of the night and heard footsteps on the floor above me. Which was interesting considering the house was a single-level home—there wasn't an upstairs.

"I'm on vacation," I insisted. "I'm not working. I'm off duty. I don't care if this house is haunted." I rolled over and put a pillow over my head and went back to sleep and didn't think about it again.

I should have.

When it came time to leave, our departure was filled with all of the chaos that can be expected from a family of five packing up a house after a ten-day stay at the beach. Anything and everything was shoved into whatever corner of the suitcase or duffel bag happened to have a spot with the idea that it would all be sorted out later.

A seasoned traveler, I am careful with my own items, like my electronics and jewelry. I don't have much jewelry, and none of it is valuable beyond sentimental reasons. When we returned home, my small travel bag of jewelry was missing. It was sentimental because it was all of the jewelry I had collected and purchased in our time abroad. I went crazy looking everywhere for it.

I knew we hadn't left it behind. That was one thing the five of us are really good at ... scouring the house to make sure there was nothing left behind. I surely would have seen my jewelry bag if I'd left it in a drawer or on a table.

Not long after we returned home, I had a meeting with Annette about her angel book. She is really good at finding lost things. I figured it would be worth asking her about it.

"Do you have any idea where my jewelry bag might be?"

She closed her eyes. "Is it a little white bag with yellow and pink flowers?"

"Yes!" I answered, excited.

She opened her eyes. "It's not here."

"What do you mean, 'it's not here'?"

"I can see a woman wearing your necklace. She's a ghost. She loves the way it shows off her cleavage."

As she said this, I could see which necklace it was and see the woman wearing it. "Seriously? A ghost stole my jewelry?"

"Yes. I guess so."

"How does that even happen?"

"It's like the dimensions shifted enough for her to get it from one to the next."

I took a minute to think about that. I had been trying to wrap my head around ascension theory metaphysical concepts and the idea that there are multiple dimensions, sometimes existing in the same space. When ghosts get stuck, they are in some sort of in-between world that seems to overlap our physical reality, so I suppose it made sense that an object could slip between these different dimensions.

"Well, will I get it back?" I asked, moving on to the more pressing question.

She shrugged. "She wants me to ask you about the cigarette. How was it?"

My eyes nearly popped out of my head. "Seriously? She saw that?"

Annette nodded.

"I was up at the Palmer House last week," I explained. "Everyone was standing outside smoking. I shared one cigarette with someone, and I can't even remember the last time I did that."

I realized this ghost had not only stolen my jewelry, but she had been following me around since Florida. I was mad.

A few weeks later, I still didn't have my jewelry back, but I had calmed down enough to want to help this ghost. I tuned in and got her story. She was a socialite from the early, glamorous days of Marco Island. She felt like she was from the '60s, and she had died of cancer. She also had several affairs with local married men and was afraid to see all of them together (not to mention their wives) if she went to heaven.

I knew exactly who to call on to help me with this one. My mom's cousin Rita was more like a sister to my mom and her brothers and sisters. She was someone we had all thought of as our own aunt. She had recently passed away from cancer at a relatively young age. If anyone knew where the hottest places to hang out and the coolest parties were in heaven, it would be my aunt Rita.

I called her in and she didn't disappoint. My aunt Rita always had a knack for becoming fast friends with anyone and everyone. She looped her arm through my Marco Island ghost and they went off together.

I still haven't gotten my jewelry back.

I have also learned that I am never on vacation, especially when I think I am on vacation.

Heaven Has Divine Helpers

Not long after the trip to Marco Island, a friend of mine reached out to me.

"My youngest, who is two, keeps talking about the ghost in her room. She tells me how the closet light—which is set to a motion sensor—turns on all by itself in the middle of the night."

"That's really cool," I said, without realizing how strange that would sound to someone who has never been on a paranormal investigation before. We use motion-sensitive lights all the time, but they hardly ever turn on. "I mean ... How scary. Want me to check it out?"

"Yes," she said. "Especially because the other night, I was lying in bed with her, and out of nowhere the light turned on. It also feels really heavy and sad in there."

"Okay, I can check in. How does the rest of the house feel?"

"There's one corner upstairs that the girls always say feels creepy. And every now and then, I feel like someone else is there with me, watching me from that corner." As she spoke, I felt like whomever she was talking about was a maid.

"Does it feel like she is judging you for doing it wrong?"

"Yes," she said. "That's exactly how it feels."

"I think that's a maid."

"Yes, that feels right."

"And I think the presence in your daughter's room is a little girl."

"Yes," she said. "That's what I think too."

"I'll let you know what I find," I said. "Do you want me to help them if they are ready to go?"

"Yes, absolutely," she said.

"Okay, I'll let you know," I said again.

As soon as I had a quiet moment, I tuned in. I instantly got the story download. The maid was actually like a nurse or nanny for the children. It felt like she worked for the first family that lived in the house.

My download told me that the family had a little girl. She got really sick and died of a fever. The maid in front of me had been blamed for the little girl's death and got fired (or perhaps she quit). She carried the guilt of the little girl's death with her for the rest of her life. She truly believed that the girl's death was her fault. When she died, she put herself in a purgatory of sorts because she didn't believe she deserved to go to heaven.

Realizing how Catholic she seemed to be, my guides suggested that I ask for special help. As a result, I humbly called on Mary to come and help me. I was hoping that seeing Mary, the mother of Jesus, would help her understand that it was okay for her to go. She was there as soon as I asked. But seeing Mary wasn't enough for this poor woman to believe that she was worthy. So I took a deep breath and asked for Jesus to come too.

And suddenly, he was standing beside me. I had to try really hard not to be in awe of the fact that Jesus was standing next to me and that he had come because I asked. It was a very humbling moment. It must have been humbling for the stubborn maid as well. As soon as the poor woman saw him, she fell into his arms and let herself be forgiven and he carried her away.

The little girl was more difficult. She was delirious when she died and it felt like she didn't know that she was dead. I couldn't really talk or reason with her. She was confused and she wasn't understanding me. One of my guides created a really big bubble of love, warmth, comfort, and clarity. She was drawn to it, and once she was standing in the middle of it, it was everything she needed to feel better. I asked my friend Megan to go with her and make sure she got to where she needed to go.

When I was done, I checked back in with the homeowner and told her everything that had happened. She walked through the house and said all of her daughters' rooms felt calm. But when she got to her youngest daughter's room, she could still feel a tingly warmth from the middle of the room. She said it almost felt "prickly."

She intentionally didn't say anything to her daughter. She wanted to see if she'd bring it up on her own. To this day, her daughter hasn't mentioned the ghost she used to talk about almost every night. She is no longer afraid of going to sleep. The light has stopped turning on by itself as well.

Through my experiences, I learned that I could call on divine helpers if I needed them. I believe that we all have spirit guides who walk alongside of us. But this experience helped me realize that we all have access to another level of guides as well. These are the ascended masters, the ones who assist a lot of people. Their energy is omnipresent and they can be many different places at the same time. They are specialty guides who often use their afterlife to continue a special purpose they began during their time on Earth. We can all access these ascended masters whenever we need them—we just have to ask.

FOUR
SPIRIT CHILDREN

Whenever I am up at the Palmer House, the ghost children follow me around. I've learned to be careful not to let them come into my room when I'm staying there. When I am there, I need to sleep. I don't need anyone waking me up all night because they want to hold my hand, even if they are children.

People often ask about child ghosts and want to know why I don't just cross them all over. The answer is because that's not my place. When someone needs my help, I know from a deep place of knowing that I am supposed to help them. The ghosts at the Palmer House are there to help people learn about the paranormal, and they have freewill choice. They have chosen this existence as their afterlife ... for now.

It's not my building; I don't own it. Any work that I do there is at the direction of the owners and the higher self of the Palmer House.

I've also come to realize that just because a ghost is showing up as a child, that doesn't necessarily mean that they died as a child. Sometimes souls choose to show up from a different time in their life. Often, they might choose a time from their childhood, when they were innocent and free.

However, if a ghost-child happens to follow me home from the Palmer House, I consider them ready to go.

I keep my house energetically protected and locked in a grid of light and love. Anything that is not light and love is simply not allowed to come in. I'm not usually too worried about anything following me home because of that protection, although that doesn't mean it hasn't happened. If something does get in through the protective grid I have around my house, I consider it a sign that I am supposed to help that soul. I trust my guides and I trust in my own abilities. If they allow something to come in, it's because I can help it.

One evening, about a week after I got back from a visit to the Palmer House, Luke (my middle son) was getting a book from the bookshelf in the hallway. He came to find me at my desk to tell me that it felt like someone poked him while he was trying to pick out a book. My own children are sensitive to energy and have shown evidence of having psychic gifts of their own. If Luke said something poked him, there was probably something there I didn't know about.

A quick psychic scan of the house told me that there might be something there. I waited for my kids to go to school the next day and then I tuned in more closely and got a download of information.

It was a little Native American boy from the Palmer House, probably about the age of nine or ten. He was the one who liked to climb into my lap when we were investigating, and I think he follows me around. He was with his friend, a little blond girl. She was younger, maybe six or seven, and had two braids. She looked like she'd just fallen out of a Laura Ingalls Wilder book. She was pale and frail and wearing a faded calico dress. I got the sense that they'd died at the same time—most likely during some sort of illness that hit Sauk Centre in the late 1800s. They were delirious and confused when they passed and didn't know what they were supposed to do after they died, so they just stayed together in their afterlife. They were best friends.

And they had decided to follow me home. I assume that because they were children (and filled with nothing but light and love), they were allowed to pass through my grid barrier. I also figured that if they followed me home, that must mean they were ready to cross over.

This was the first time a ghost was in my actual physical "space," as evidenced by my son getting poked, and not just in my mind's eye. It definitely made everything more real. It made me realize I must have a lot of extra protection and layers if I could go a few days at home and not even notice they were there until my son pointed it out. It also made me aware that I needed to be more careful and more intentional. If my kids were picking up on something I wasn't, that meant I wasn't as tuned in as I thought (or maybe had a harder time reaching through my extra layers of protection to be able to know).

I wasn't quite sure what to do with the two child ghosts: what did they need to see or understand before they could cross over? Mac and Megan had been helpful at the house clearing, so I reached out to them to see if they could help me now. They both came right away. Mac took the little boy's hand, and Megan reached for the little girl. Together, the four of them walked off through a tunnel and into the light.

After they were gone, I sat there and cried. In the moment, I defined them as tears of gratitude. But I've also come to realize that sometimes, after helping a soul find its way to heaven, my physical body can't process the overwhelming unconditional love. Not able to contain that love in my physical body, it releases through the act of crying.

I had so much gratitude that these two little souls had finally found their way to heaven after such a long time of being lost. I was also grateful that Mac and Megan were there to help me when I needed it. I was beginning to think of Mac and Megan as my "dead crew" and I was so happy and appreciative for their help.

A Lost Little Girl from the Great Depression

Not long after, I was back at the Palmer House. There were several of us there to help out for an event. At one point on Saturday afternoon, we went down to the basement to help set up equipment. But we had a little bit of fun investigating too.

The paranormal team from a local Minnesota group, Things That Go Bump, was coordinating the investigation for the weekend. My friends John and Ryan founded the group. Over the years, I found myself frequently working with them at the Palmer House.

I was in one of the back basement rooms with Grant, one of their team members. It's a room where I've always felt a lot of gangster and prohibition party energy. We were playing with a Mel Meter (a device used to detect a change in electromagnetic frequency).

We think we were interacting with one of the gangsters. Whoever it was, he was being very playful. Grant moved the meter and let it hover over a chair. The light and sound went off, indicating the ghost had sat in a chair.

"Great," said Grant. "Now try this one."

He moved the meter to the next chair.

Moments later, the light and sound went off again, indicating the ghost had followed his device.

This continued another twelve to fifteen times and each time, the light would go off and the sound would buzz.

We were laughing and joking. Excited to share our experience with the others, we went down to a room we call the Snowman Room to tell them. (We call it the Snowman Room because it's where the infamous Palmer House Snowman—an antique, life-size snowman that is known to move its arms and turn its head even though the electric pieces stopped working ages ago—is kept when it's not in the lobby for the winter.) Everyone was sitting in the chairs, which were arranged in a circle.

I felt a rush of energy enter the room with us. It was a feeling that I associate with the younger, child spirits of the Palmer

House. We sat down, and not long after, we felt like child ghosts were climbing all over everyone.

But it wasn't long before the energy changed. A little ghost girl came into the room. Some of those in the room could see her, her energy was that strong. (I wasn't one of them. Although, if I closed my eyes, I got an image in my head of what she looked like.) She was about six or seven with a short blond bob that looked like someone had cut it at home. She was dirty and wearing a dress right out of the Depression. This little girl wasn't playful. This little girl was sad, alone, and lost.

"I need to find my mom," she said. Her words were so clear that we captured them in an EVP.

EVP is short for electronic voice phenomena. Paranormal investigators use an audio recorder during an investigation to help record what is happening. The equipment has the capability to pick up sounds that aren't always heard with human ears. Upon replaying the audio from a ghost hunt in a haunted location, we will often pick up disembodied voices answering our questions.

The little girl stood by John, one of the co-founders from Things That Go Bump.

"I need to find my mom," she said again.

I was overwhelmed with her sadness to the point where I almost started to cry just to help release it.

She climbed onto John's lap. Her energy was so strong some people in the room could even see her arm stretch out and go around his neck.

I got the sense that he reminded her of her grandfather. I repeated this out loud and others agreed.

The whole time she was with us, I kept thinking to myself, *Someone should help her. Why isn't anyone helping her?*

And then I heard a voice in my head say, *You. That someone is you. You are supposed to help her.*

I was a little overwhelmed. I had never done anything like this out loud before—I had never done anything like this in front of other people. I took a deep breath.

"Okay," I said. "We need to help her."

But I couldn't think of anything. I couldn't think of what to do for her. But I knew that Mac and Megan had been available before to help me with little kids. I asked if Megan could come to help me.

"I know someone I can call to help you," I told her. "My friend Megan is really good at finding people. She can help you find your people."

Megan was there with me as soon as I said her name out loud. She reached out and took the little girl's hand.

But then I wasn't sure what to do. I had a sudden, strong understanding that I couldn't just help her the way I would normally help someone. I couldn't call a big ball of light into the middle of the Palmer House or wrap her up in a bubble in the basement because it would be too disruptive to the other ghost energies.

Instead, my guides showed me a tunnel. It looked almost like a mining tunnel. It went out of the basement and down around the corner. There was a warm, glowing light at the end of it.

Before I could say anything, someone else in the room said, "I can see a tunnel."

Together, Megan and the little girl walked into the tunnel and disappeared around the corner.

"I can see them walking down a tunnel and into a light," someone else said.

There was a swirl of energy and she was gone.

Not All Ghosts Are Dead

I was called in to clear a space. My client was having a problem in one of the bedrooms. Oftentimes, the light in the closet would turn on in the middle of the night all by itself. It was especially strange that the light switch for the closet was on the outside of the closet door ... in the bedroom.

When I tuned in to scan the space, I wasn't prepared for the images I saw. I could see a little girl trapped in the closet. The download of information that came with the images told me that she had been locked in the closet many, many times for misbehaving. When she was inside the closet, she was left in the dark. This was especially terrifying for her because she was afraid of the dark. But because the light switch was outside of the closet, there was nothing she could do about it.

Unfortunately, experience had taught me on previous visits that this house was notoriously haunted. While it was much clearer and more stable now, at the time this little girl had been locked in the closet, there was a lot of energy moving in, around, and through the whole house. This poor little girl had a very good reason to be afraid of the dark—she was sensitive enough to know that when she was locked in the dark closet, she was never locked in there alone.

My guides showed me that she was the ghost responsible for turning on the light in the closet. She never wanted that closet to be dark. If she had a chance to turn the light on, no matter what time of the night it was, she was going to turn it on.

There was just one thing. When I asked how to help the little girl and if she was ready to go to heaven, my guides showed me a grown woman who was still alive. This little girl's soul wasn't actually dead.

But something was turning on the closet light. There was something intelligent interacting in the same time and space by turning on the closet light any chance it could. If this intelligent energy was part of that woman's soul, and that woman hadn't yet died, then this was a sliver of her soul that seemed to have been left behind—interacting with the human world as if it were a ghost.

Through this experience I learned that sometimes when a soul experiences trauma, as a matter of self-preservation, that soul can splice part of itself—the part that experienced the trauma—out. That splinter of soul is left behind as a way for the rest of the soul to keep moving forward. This interaction with the little girl and the closet light taught me that the sliver of a soul that gets left behind can have an intelligent interaction with the human world. That splinter of a soul can interact intelligently in the same way a ghost can interact intelligently.

In this situation, instead of helping that sliver of a soul cross over and move on to heaven, I wrapped it up and sent it back to its higher self, asking that the sliver be healed and reunited with the woman. After this, the closet light stopped turning on all by itself.

Cape Man and His Mother

Another recurring ghost sighting from the Palmer House Hotel involved a large, dark shadow man ... with a cape. This energy had been seen in the laundry room and in the basement. He seemed to like scaring and startling people, and often he seemed to have a little boy with him who would laugh when people got scared. The shadow man seemed to be growing bigger and stronger.

The download of information that came in when I heard this story took me back to an interview we had done with my Ghost Stories Ink group for our documentary. A friend and colleague of mine, Eric Christopher, offers past life regression therapy. My crew of guides told me that our interview with Eric was the key to understanding Cape Man's motivations.

In the interview, Eric told the story of a past life regression session in which his client remembered being a ghost. During this session, his client (under hypnosis) described a life in long-ago England. This man died violently. He was in a loveless arranged marriage and had gotten into an argument with his wife. They were standing at the top of the steps. She pushed him and he fell backward down the staircase, breaking his neck. As he lay dying, she leaned over him and whispered a confession: she'd been having an affair with his best friend. He died so angry that he remained stuck in the house to haunt the property.

He recalled how he would intentionally try to scare people just to get an energy boost from their fear. He described how this fear seemed to feed him and make him stronger. He described time periods changing quickly, which he would mark by the different styles of dress. He described how his appearance had changed from that of a man to more of a gargoyle's features and appearance. He explained that it was what we would describe as a "demon" if we saw it. The man explained that he would sometimes get bored and go outside to sit on the country hillside. Every so often, he would feel like something was trying to pull him up. But he would always resist that pull until one day, he gave in and was pulled up to heaven.

My guides showed me how the Cape Man was using a similar tactic: he was scaring people just to get an energy boost. But he also had another motive—he was trying to make the little boy with him laugh. Because this Cape Man seemed to be growing larger and stronger, his strategy to feed off fear seemed to be working.

My download of information provided me with some additional, personal details about this particular story. He had lived in the mid- to late-1800s. Cape Man's mother had died, leaving him orphaned at a young age. This was not an easy time to be an orphan on the prairie. Cape Man had an extremely rough life and had been abused in multiple ways. In his adult life, he became part of a traveling circus and wore a cape. He loved the power his role in the circus provided him, and he loved the adrenaline rush he would get from scaring people.

I shared all of this information and background with Kelley, the owner of the Palmer House. We sat in the pub and talked. We talked about how hard his life must have been and how much compassion we felt for him. We talked about how horrible it must have been to be an orphan at that time in history. The more we talked about all of this, the more I could feel his power shrink. Because we simply acknowledged the harshness of his situation, he seemed to lose the need and desire for power.

Later that night, I was startled awake around 3:00 a.m. As I was going back to sleep, I got an additional download from Cape Man's mother. When she died, she hadn't wanted to leave her little boy. Instead of going to heaven, she'd vowed to stay by his side. He grew up without knowing or having any idea that she was still right beside him, trying to help him. She had stayed at a low vibration because she hadn't wanted to leave his side.

He had grown more angry and more horrible with each passing year. He died a miserable and lonely death, but because of his anger and rage, he couldn't see her. After he died, she finally gave up on him and went to the light. But now, he was the one at the low vibration who was lost and confused.

He had a little boy with him. But this little boy, his mother explained, was actually a younger version of himself. It was like he had wanted to keep the part of himself that was innocent and free separate from his evil and pain. He had splintered off that part of himself to try to save it. The Cape Man had fun entertaining his little-boy self by scaring people. And every time he scared people and the little boy laughed, Cape Man grew bigger and stronger.

The Cape Man could hear his mother telling me all of this and he shrunk again, this time from embarrassment and shame. At the time, I should have explained that he didn't have to carry the guilt from this, but it didn't occur to me. He was in awe that his mother was there, and he was distracted by her presence. He probably wouldn't have even heard me.

It felt like the situation needed to settle for a few days. Meanwhile, that gave me time to share the rest of the story with Kelley and ask her what she wanted me to try to do with Cape Man and the little boy if they were still there. However, after a few days, I checked in and the situation had resolved itself. I didn't need to do anything. I think because his mother was at a higher vibration, she was able to take care of him and help him get to where he was supposed to go. He was over-whelmed that she'd stayed by him for so long, and her love and forgiveness were all he needed to find his way.

The fact that this situation resolved itself on its own reassured me that I wasn't making it up. If I had been making it up, my ego would have insisted that I be a part of the story's resolution. In any event, it was a good reminder that sometimes something scary just needs a little love and forgiveness.

FIVE
EVIL SPIRITS

October is typically a pretty busy month for a paranormal author and investigator. It's the month of the year when everyone wants to talk about ghosts. Jessica and I had a book coming out, which made it even busier. We were trying to schedule a book signing at a local liquor store because the owner wanted to do some sort of "wine and sign." On top of all that, we also had an event happening at the Palmer House Hotel.

On my way out of town, I stopped by the liquor store to let the owner know that our book had been released and that we could schedule a signing anytime. I felt bad going into the store just to talk about the book without buying anything, so I purchased a six-pack of my favorite hard cider and tucked it away in the car.

Jessica and I were able to leave before rush hour, so the drive went by quickly. There was a charged anticipation that seemed to hang in the air. It was always fun and exciting to head up to the Palmer House for an event, but this felt different.

It was almost like I could sense the urgent energy of the hotel all the way there (and now that I know more, looking back, that's exactly what it was). Something was wrong, and the resident ghosts needed help.

From the first few minutes in the hotel, we knew something was off. We were staying in Lucy's room, as usual. When I opened the door, the fragrance was overpowering. Lucy often makes herself known by her perfume ... if she likes you. The best way to describe it is a mix between flowers and baby powder, not unlike Love's Baby Soft scents.

"Do you smell that?" I asked Jessica. "It smells really strong, like perfume. Is that Lucy's perfume smell?"

Jessica shrugged. "I'm not sure. Let's remember to ask how long ago the room was cleaned. It could be cleaning solution."

"Maybe," I said. But I didn't think so. It was too floral—too perfume-y.

"I've got to go get a bag from my car," said Jessica, turning to go back out in the hall.

I stayed to settle in. Realizing I'd accidentally brought the cider with me from the car, I tucked it away in the small fridge. I'd meant to leave it in the car and take it home again.

When Jessica came back, she hurried into the room and closed the door.

"What's wrong?" I asked.

She leaned against the door but didn't answer right away. After a few seconds she said, "I'm not sure. The hallway felt strange. It feels off here."

"What do you mean?"

"I was fiddling with the door, and I felt like something was watching me from all the way down the hall. And then suddenly, it was right next to me and it felt really creepy and I couldn't get in here fast enough. But it feels fine in here."

"Huh," I said. "That is strange."

It went on to be a strange weekend. My new computer kept crashing—it had never crashed before and has never crashed since. I was mostly working on edits for my client's book about angels. The significance of that grew more poignant as the weekend went on. We tried to download software onto Jessica's computer for a new ghost-hunting gadget (an adapted camera that can map images onto a screen) that we were excited to try—it never worked, and her computer kept crashing too.

It wasn't just our computers. My own energy felt drained as well. I was exhausted all weekend. Sometimes, I feel like the Palmer House exists in what seems to be a whole different (or even multiple) dimensions of time and space. Whenever I am at the Palmer House, I try to get out of the building over the course of my stay to rebalance my own energy. Often, I do so by going for a run and it grounds me. Feeling my feet pound on the pavement helps me reset my soul and anchor my energy back into the earth.

But getting out of the building felt especially important that weekend. When I did, I was compelled to stay out longer than usual. And for the first time ever, I was pulled to run a route past the Catholic church. As I did, a song came on my playlist that I associate as my fight song. Whenever I hear it, it usually signifies that a battle of some sort is brewing.

I walked back into the Palmer House with angels at my side, ready to face whatever it might be. Little did I know what was coming.

That night, our investigation was off. The ghosts interacted, but not like usual. Usually, we get a lot of flashlight activity and capture some good EVPs. We typically use mini Maglites set at a hair trigger. Ghosts, especially at the Palmer House, have figured out how to manipulate a flashlight to be able to answer yes and no questions. Our Palmer House events usually have a lot of flashlight activity that answers our questions and EVPs that provide our attendees with some good paranormal evidence. But none of that happened this time. The flashlights went off, but not in a way that seemed intelligent.

Our attendees seemed more skeptical than past groups and were less willing to try to interact. I found myself working much harder to lead a group than I usually have to. The ghosts seemed to be off as well. We seemed to get just enough interaction that the ghosts were letting us know they were there, but they didn't want to play or interact. My psychic self confirmed this. Something was clearly wrong.

It's interesting to note that our group of attendees was the smallest we'd ever had. It was just big enough not to cancel the event, but smaller than we had done in the past. Now, looking back, it seems as though the universe had planned for that intentionally.

At the end of the night, anyone who was still awake wanted to go back down into the basement. I really just wanted to go to bed, but I absolutely knew that I needed to be down in that basement. We sat in the Snowman Room, our chairs in a circle.

Our group was quiet. No one was willing to participate too much—and while it was just like we had been dealing with over the entire course of the evening, it was very out of character for typical Palmer House groups.

There was a woman at the end of the room who was sitting near the door and her chair was positioned in a way that she could see down the hall. Finally, she mentioned she could see a dark shadow low to the ground. The Palmer family children used to keep their dogs in the basement. Over the course of our many visits, we've gotten great thermal imaging photos of dog shapes, EVPs of dogs barking, and people who even felt and sensed dogs moving around their legs. Everyone in the room started calling for the dog to come in.

"Here puppy, come here," said someone.

I looked at Jessica in the dark. Her eyes narrowed at me and the look in them told me she was thinking the same thing I was. Without even saying a word, we both agreed that whatever the dark shadow was, it wasn't a dog. I knew it from that deep place of knowing, and I knew we had to keep our group safe from whatever it was.

I closed my eyes and asked Archangel Michael to stand at the doorway. I always invoke extra protection on behalf of our attendees when our evening starts, but I reinforced it now. I extended the bubble of protection that I use during an investigation and pushed it out to cover our whole group by calling on their higher selves for consent. I reinforced the protective barriers of the room, visualizing energy grids surrounding us. I knew, without a doubt, that whatever was out in the hallway would not be able to come into the Snowman Room. Nor would it want to with the angels I'd asked to stand guard at the door.

Together, our group kept everyone laughing and light-hearted. We had some flashlight activity happening in the room, so we concentrated on that. Later, in the car on the way home, Jessica and I listened for EVPs from the voice recorder we had running the whole time. Whenever the room swelled with laughter, an EVP with a woman's voice repeated, "Go home, go home, go home." It was like she was using the energy from our laughter to whisper her warning.

The night ended without incident, and I have never been so thankful to be finished with an investigation. Afterward, Jessica and I invited McCann, our teammate, to our room. After all, I had a six-pack of hard cider that I'd accidentally brought with me. It's interesting to note that with all of our previous events, we had never really hung out after. It just wasn't something we would've normally done. Usually, we were so exhausted after a day of teaching classes followed by an investigation that we all just went to bed. But because we happened to have the cider from my stop on the way out of town, and because our night had felt so off, it made sense that we would take a minute together to process it.

Jessica and I (and it seemed, Lucy) invited McCann in for a cider. He sat down in Lucy's chair. Lucy doesn't like when anyone sits in her chair—and she especially doesn't like when men sit in her chair. But on this night, I could feel that she was excited we were all there together. I even felt as though she offered her chair to McCann. She absolutely didn't care that he was sitting there, she was just happy that we were all there to talk about how our night had gone. In fact, it felt like all of the unregistered guests in the hotel were standing in a line outside our door.

We put the pieces of our night together, concluding that the ghosts really wanted us to know that something was off. We laughed about the fact that our group was trying to willingly call what was probably a demon dog into the middle of the room. We also talked about how we knew, without a doubt, there was no way that presence could get past the barriers Jessica and I had built to keep everyone in the room safe.

When we finished talking, it felt like everyone (the ghosts) out in the hallway were cheering and wanted to give us a high five for figuring it out.

After we got home, I spoke with Kelley, consulted with one of my mentors, and started working remotely to do whatever I could to help the Palmer House. When I was tuning in to the Palmer House to try to figure out what this energy was and what we should do about it, I realized this entity was splintering off pieces of itself and sticking them into the energetic layers of people with weak auras.

During this same time period, I had to meet with Annette, my angel book client, about her book. She helped to validate some of the things I was picking up on. But I will never forget her words of advice: "If you are going to work on this, and do work like this, you absolutely have to believe in yourself. You're going to have to pull on your big girl pants and get it done. There is no room for doubt."

She was absolutely right. From what I know about negative entities, especially of this sort, there can be no doubt. Any little opening of self-doubt gives that entity room to move into my field. Over time, I have learned to have complete trust and faith in my guides and angels. I have faith in them that I am thoroughly protected. I have also learned to trust that the universe will only bring me what I can handle. If something ends up in front of me, I know I can handle it or it wouldn't have shown up.

To this day, if I am faced with a new challenge or something that pushes me to the limits of what I know, I hear Annette's voice in my head instructing me. "It's time to pull on your big girl pants."

Whenever I am clearing anyone or anything, the first thing I do is connect to the higher self of whomever I am working with. If I am working with a person, that's their higher self. If I am working with a space, I connect with the higher self of the space. I ask that the higher self direct everything that we talk about and everything that I do. It's a way to keep my ego (and what I want to have happen) completely out of the picture. It's not about me—it's about what is in the greatest and highest good of whomever or whatever I am working with.

I spent two days of meditation looking for this energy's splinters and pulling them out of people. There were a few people whose higher self denied me access to work with them. I am assuming that I was denied access because there was some lesson those people needed to learn on their own from this experience. In those cases, there was nothing I could do but move on to the next.

When I would find a splinter, I would visualize plucking it out of the aura it had been stuck in and wrapping it up in a bubble of its own. Then I set the intention and asked that this bubble be sent off to a higher dimension of light and love so that whatever was inside could evolve into its next highest level.

When I was finished, I was left with an incredible concept for a horror novel that I couldn't have made up if I tried. I started working on it the very next week.

I was up to the Palmer House again a few weeks later for another event. The best part of that weekend was realizing that the demon dog was gone.

An Evil Presence in Paradise

One February, one of my mentors reached out about a property that she and her colleague had tried to clear but couldn't quite seem to get. It was a property that had been purchased with the dream of turning it into a vacation retreat in a tropical paradise somewhere in Mexico. I was signed up to attend a workshop with her, and she requested that everyone work together remotely by all tuning in at the same time on a designated day. She sent everyone a photo of the property.

I got a nudge to tune in to the property in advance just to see what was there. In my meditation, I could see the sprawling, beautiful property—that was haunted by a very dark, sweeping, evil presence. I could also see a little chapel, and in it was the ghost of a priest who was desperately trying to help keep the property safe from the dark presence—or so he thought. He had come to the land after the evil, and he truly believed with his whole heart that he had cleared the evil presence away. He then "sacrificed himself and his eternity in heaven" (his words) by choosing to instead stay at the property to "protect" the land and keep the dark entity from coming back.

Only this dark presence had actually played him and tricked him (and more importantly, his ego) into making him *think* that's what he was doing. The evil entity was actually using him as a bridge of sorts to lock on to the land. It somehow knew that his presence and refusal to cross was actually helping it, because the priest was constantly interfering with any lightwork meant to heal the land. Because the priest had never crossed over, he was functioning at a lower vibration that ultimately kept him confused and ineffective. If he had crossed over, he would have been at a higher vibration that would have allowed him to see through the different dimensions. The dark presence had tricked him into protecting it on his behalf.

My guides even showed me how the entity would stage battles with him every now and then, just to make him think he was still being effective in keeping the property safe. They also showed me that the priest was an absolute expert at avoiding any attempts to get him to cross over or make him leave. He knew how to make himself invisible and step away whenever any lightwork was attempted. He also deliberately tried to sabotage any efforts to clear the property. All of this proved to me that freewill choice can be a powerful thing.

I knew, from that deep place of knowing, that the only way to successfully clear the property was to convince the priest to cross over ... and that wasn't going to be easy. There was also a strange pattern of energy emanating from the energetic infrastructure of the Catholic church that was locking him down and essentially keeping him trapped there. It was interfering with his freewill choice by not allowing him to see the true picture.

The more I tuned in, the more clearly I could see the priest as he truly was, and it looked to me like he barely had a soul left. It looked like it was full of dark holes, like it had been almost completely eaten away by the evil. It suddenly felt as though time was of the essence. This poor soul was about to be completely consumed by the evil that had invaded this land.

I sent a note to my mentor to tell her about the information I had picked up. Sitting down to write that email took a lot of courage. Typing everything out in black and white was fully admitting the crazy going on inside my head: "Hello ... there is a tormented soul locked in by an evil presence ..."

But after the thing that I had worked on in the basement of the Palmer House, I tried not to think too much about how crazy it sounded and instead focused on giving an accurate account of my psychic download. I assumed that if I was getting the information about the priest, that meant I was supposed to try to help him.

In writing that email, I learned to detach from any expectation of the outcome. I felt like I needed to relay facts and pieces of the story that I had picked up on just in case it helped someone else with the work they were feeling called to do. But when I clicked "send," I also completely detached from needing to know anything that happened after that. I knew what my work and my piece of the situation was supposed to be, and no one needed to know any part of it unless my mentor felt called to share.

But for some reason, my dead crew was telling me that I needed to wait two days to try to talk to him. I wasn't entirely sure why. Maybe I just needed to let it percolate in my own mind to make sure I knew what I was doing. Also, two days away was Thursday and if I was successful, that would give the property two more days to settle before the group attempted their collective remote clearing on Saturday. I've learned that there is something magical about letting things settle for two days with respect to the metaphysical world.

My guides told me to brush up on my Spanish, then laughed. I actually got a little worried that there could be a potential language barrier. But then they said, "Just kidding. We'll get you an interpreter. But it would be good if you could use a few words from that Spanish minor." (My guides have a funny sense of humor.)

Thursday morning arrived. I went to the property the same way I went to the Palmer House kitchen—I meditated, encircled myself with protection, and imagined myself walking through the door of the chapel my guides had told me was on the property.

Having been raised in Catholic schools and being a Catholic myself, I understood his faith. I understood what this priest was trying to do and what he thought he was accomplishing. I also knew that if I asked Archangel Michael to come with, I would be safe. I also had the thought to ask Mary to join me— it was as if my guides suggested that seeing her would be good for the priest. I humbly asked her to come. When she showed up, I tried not to be in awe of the fact that she was standing next to me. I figured that if this poor priest saw Archangel Michael and the Mother Mary with me, the true part that was still his soul would be drawn to come talk to me.

I went to sit down in the back pew of the chapel.

Within a few minutes, the priest was there, and he was curious enough to come talk to me. With Mary by my side, I explained, "You've served your time here on Earth. The angels are calling you to go be with them in heaven."

He didn't say anything, but I knew he didn't believe me.

I continued. "You've done a good job. But the angels know you are really tired of fighting. It's okay to leave now."

I could feel his resolve to stay start to weaken.

"They want you to go to a place now where you can rest and recover."

"But that will mean that I failed," he finally said.

"No, it doesn't. It means that you've done your duty."

I knew he wanted with his whole heart to believe me, but I wasn't sure if he really did.

I took a chance and called in a bubble of light. He went into it reluctantly but willingly. I could feel his exhaustion.

However, once he got inside the bubble, he second-guessed himself and was overwhelmed with guilt. It was almost like the bubble provided a clarity he had been missing for a long time. Feeling the need to punish himself because of it, he envisioned himself bursting into flames because he still didn't feel like he deserved to be there.

Instantly, I tried to counter it by visualizing snow filling his bubble to put out the fire. My guides were showing me how to literally help him chill out. He collapsed, exhausted, and the bubble floated off, taking him to a place of peace.

Before I left the property, I tuned in and scanned the rest of the area to see if there was anything else I needed to do. I was surprised to find an entire group of lost souls huddled in the corner of what looked to me to be a mining pit or a deep hole of some sort. They were cowering together against the wall, afraid to come out and afraid to move. My guides helped me open up a tunnel of light in the wall, and they all hurried through it and crossed to safety.

On Saturday I was at an indoor soccer tournament in Kansas City. I wasn't able to tune in to the collective meditation with the rest of the group at the agreed-upon time. However, my mentor emailed everyone the following week to report that the property was finally as peaceful as it had ever been.

After this experience I learned that when I work with the bubble concept, it is good to ask and set the intent that the inside of the bubble offers not just clarity, but support and understanding as well. I now set the intention that the soul inside will feel better and safe and that the bubble will provide anything else they need to feel in order to feel peace about their decision to cross over and go to the light.

SIX

TROUBLEMAKERS

Not long ago, a famous psychic went through the Palmer House and identified an interesting ghost entity in the basement. This ghost was quite literally picking on people. He would reach through the wall and try to peel off layers of their energy. New (and/or underdeveloped) empaths seemed to be the most at risk. The ghost's murdered wife was also involved. He had killed her. She was angry about having been murdered, and she didn't like men. Any time her husband would come out of the woodwork and his hiding spot in the corner, she would fly in from the other side of the basement to attack him. As a result, he had tried to build layer upon layer of protection around himself, almost as if he were trying to camouflage himself. In my mind, I visualized it as if he was a swamp man in a ghillie suit.

The psychic provided recommendations and advice about how to deal with the husband and wife. Kelley took the information and conversation seriously and was determined to do whatever she needed to do to keep the basement—and all of the Palmer House—safe for both the registered and unregistered guests. As she likes to say, "Anyone is allowed to stay as long as they play by the rules."

Not long after that happened, I was up at the Palmer House again to help with a big event that was to include a paranormal investigation in the basement. The Empath Eater (as we had started to call him) was still there. As with any basement tour of the Palmer House Hotel, there were sure to be vulnerable empaths in the group, going down to investigate in that very same basement.

I stationed myself downstairs. At one point, a group came and sat along the wall to the room where the Empath Eater liked to hide. When one of our group members mentioned that it felt like something pinched his cheek, I knew I had to do something.

I didn't want to scare anyone with a big announcement, so I tried to contain the ghost in a bubble. But it didn't work. His own freewill choice wouldn't allow for it. Instead, I connected to the higher selves of everyone in the room, pulled in the higher self of the Palmer House Hotel, and went to work making a giant bubble of protection around the group.

We were having a lot of activity with the child spirits of the hotel and I didn't want them to leave. I made the giant bubble look like a circus tent so the little ones wouldn't be afraid.

We got through the night without further incident, but we wrapped up the third group a little early. By then, I was exhausted.

———

The next week, I found myself thinking about the Empath Eater a lot. I wondered what would cause someone to try to peel layers off of empaths in particular. Coincidentally (or not), every time I thought about the Empath Eater, a song popped into my head—John Lennon's "All You Need Is Love." I started to feel really bad for the Empath Eater. It seemed to me that the reason he was stealing energy from empaths was because he was trying to steal "love."

I started thinking that maybe that really *was* all he needed. He was obviously looking for something specific by picking on empaths. If I could pull some of my helpers together, maybe we could come up with exactly the thing that this poor soul was looking for ... love, forgiveness, and understanding. Maybe we could make a big ball of love and use it like bait. The Empath Eater could try it, it would be exactly what he was looking for, and I would be able to talk him into going where he needed to go.

I knew I was physically prepared to handle the Empath Eater. By this time, my guides had upgraded my personal protective shield. Now, instead of a bubble, I thought of a square around my body and I anchored it to the four directions—north, south, east, and west. The walls ran the length of my body, and at the top of my head, triangles folded to a point. The same thing happened at my feet. The top tip joined with a divine connection, and the tip on the bottom stretched down to anchor in the earth. It looked like a prism shark cage made out of energy, and it was impenetrable. So much so that when I did a scanning exercise with a partner during a psychic development weekend, my partner couldn't physically get her hands past my protection no matter how hard she pushed, and I wasn't even trying to keep her out. It has since shifted again, to be something even more geometrical. It seems that as the work that I do shifts, my guides help me shift the tools and methods I use to keep my energy field safe.

———————

I found a quiet place and tuned in remotely. My team had the big ball of love ready, with contributions from every dimension to make sure it was just what he needed. They put it in the middle of the room on the other side of the wall where the Empath Eater hid. I blocked off everything else in the hotel so nothing and no one else knew it was happening, especially his poor murdered wife.

Within minutes, I saw his arm reach through the wall and peel off a layer from the ball. I watched as he made contact. Instantly, his face and all of his emotions told me this was exactly what he'd been looking for, and for the first time in his afterlife, he was completely satisfied. He looked up and realized I was there.

"What is it?" he asked.

As he asked the question, I got a download about his life. It had been filled with hardship and tragedy.

"You've had a really hard and terrible life," I said. "You don't need to stay here anymore. You can go somewhere where you feel like *that* all of the time," I said pointing to the ball in the middle of the room.

He looked at it.

"I know you're trying to steal love from anyone and everyone. But you don't have to steal it. You are allowed to go somewhere where you always feel that love, forgiveness, and understanding."

"How?" he asked.

I called in a bubble that was filled with everything he needed.

Without so much as a single word, he jumped inside of it. Instantly, I could feel how tired he was. But even more important, I could feel his relief. He was relieved to finally find what he'd spent so long looking for.

He was gone within minutes. I lifted the energy of invisibility I'd been using. It didn't take long for his wife to come looking for him—she came flying in from the other side of the basement.

I told her he was gone and he was never coming back. She didn't have to worry about him ever again. With my words, she flopped down, exhausted. I could see her in a field of wild-flowers by a mountain stream. She was already ready to go, so I wrapped her up in her own bubble of light and love and sent her on her way.

Looking back, I realize I barely even had to do anything. All I did was acknowledge they both had a really tough life, offer them both love and understanding, and help them get to a place where they could feel forgiveness and acceptance. I think the whole thing only took about fifteen minutes.

I was overwhelmed. Fifteen minutes of love, forgiveness, and understanding wiped away a lifetime of hardship, anger, hatred, and guilt. It made me think that if we all spent fifteen minutes each day focused on love, acceptance, and understanding... maybe we could change the world.

Skeletor the Skeleton Man

Recently, the Palmer House Hotel was featured on the Travel Channel's show *The Dead Files*. It was fascinating to watch a television episode about a location that I am so familiar with. Watching the show made me realize that not everyone's psychic gifts work the same.

There was a ghost at the Palmer House who made it into the show, and they even provided a professional sketch drawn by an artist. This sketch was terrifying. The man in it was wearing a full suit, and his skeleton head was not unlike the evil character named Skeletor in the He-Man cartoon series my brothers used to watch. Looking at it made me feel like I had reached into the depths of my childhood. In the sketch, he was quite literally strong-arming a real person, who was screaming in terror.

The first time I watched the Palmer House episode of *The Dead Files*, that sketched image burned into my brain and locked itself into my memory. I had never seen that ghost at the Palmer House. I hadn't ever heard about anything like that happening there. My ego went straight to a conclusion—if I hadn't seen it, then it must not still be there.

As a psychic, ego can be a very dangerous thing.

I work hard to walk a fine line with ego in my work. I need enough ego to believe in myself and be confident in my abilities. Otherwise, I will fail. I wouldn't be able to do this work without confidence. But too much ego easily gets in the way. Just because I have this "gift" doesn't mean that I am the only one who can do the work. I am not the only one with answers, and my answers might very well be different than someone else's.

Psychic gifts work differently for different people. No two psychics are the same, so there is no reason to assume their gifts would work the same way. When I first started doing this work, if I couldn't "see," "feel," "hear," or "know" the exact same information in the exact same way someone else might be "seeing," "feeling," "hearing," or "knowing" it, it was really easy for me to think that I was "doing it wrong." It took me a while to realize that different is not wrong.

My gift works at a different vibration. In the beginning, this made me feel inadequate. I felt like I was "doing it wrong" because my gifts weren't working the same as someone else's. But now I embrace it. I love to work with my friend Nicole because her gifts work differently than mine. It's almost like we each "see" different pieces of the puzzle. By working together, we see more of the whole picture.

This can also go the other way. Just because I am getting different information than someone else does not, in any way, make my information "better" or "worse." The second I find myself labeling and judging the information coming in as "good" or "bad" or "better" or "worse," I know that my ego is getting in the way. This is also one of the reasons I like to diversify my teachers and mentors. I've learned something from all of them, but their gifts work differently from each other and are different from mine.

I've also learned to accept that it's okay to make mistakes. Making mistakes is actually part of the process. We are all divine beings, but we are living on Earth as human beings. Humans, by their very nature, make mistakes. We are all here, in this lifetime, to learn lessons. We can't learn those lessons without making a few mistakes. Our souls are here for a specific purpose and to have a unique opportunity to learn and grow. We can't do that if we don't mess up once in a while. We can't grow without failure and the chance to rise up to try again.

I've made a few mistakes.

In February, there was an event at the Palmer House that required a lot of extra helping hands. There were going to be a lot of guests in attendance, all moving through the hotel throughout the evening for a paranormal investigation. Several of us were on hand to help move groups through the investigation and to help answer any questions that might come up, especially about the Palmer House.

We also make sure the energy in the building is good to go for a paranormal investigation. This often means walking through the building and trying to get a sense of the areas that would be good to investigate—and sometimes, figuring out which rooms to avoid. Jenny (a good friend of mine from the Palmer House) and I were walking through the hotel before everyone arrived. As we were focusing on this task, an attendee who had been staying at the hotel—and investigating on his own in the public areas of the hotel—mentioned that he felt an irritated, angry presence in one of the rooms upstairs.

"Do you think it could be the skeleton man from the *Dead Files* sketch?" he asked.

"No," I answered quickly.

"We think he left with someone," Jenny added.

We went upstairs to check out the room he had mentioned. Jenny and I both agreed the room felt off... and angry.

"We're going to be doing an investigation tonight," Jenny explained to the air.

"If you don't want anyone to bother you," I said, "there will be rooms in the basement you can hang out in and we won't let anyone go in there."

"Or you can go to my room," said Jenny.

"Or mine," I added.

I was staying in the room we call "the apartment." There had been some pretty wonky energy in this room for a while and we had been trying to balance it out for a long time. People staying in this room often reported being startled awake by a male presence, which they then felt staring at them. The closet light regularly turned on inexplicably. Also, the television was known to spontaneously turn on in the middle of the night for no earthly reason.

None of this would ever happen when I stayed in this space. I felt protected when I stayed there. Every time I stayed in the apartment, I would focus on balancing the energy within it, trying to harmonize it with the whole of the building.

We focused on doing this work slowly, over time. I've learned the hard way that trying to raise the vibration of a space too quickly can be uncomfortable for those who have to live and function in the space. Now, I always try to set the intention that any vibrational energy work that I am doing in a space will happen at a level all affected souls can tolerate.

Some time later, I was doing a reading for a client in the apartment. As the reading was wrapping up, my arm started to hurt. I felt pain from my shoulder down through my elbow, almost like someone had twisted my arm up behind my back. It was odd, because I obviously hadn't been doing anything physical with my arm for the last few hours that would possibly be able to explain why it hurt.

Later that night, during our event, I was down in the basement. All of the event participants had been divided into groups. During one of the transition periods when the groups were shifting, there were a few people who had gotten distracted and wandered off into one of the rooms that was supposed to be off limits. It happened to be the same room where we had told our angry friend he could hide out and not be disturbed. I worried about him as I helped the group get back on track and closed the door to the back room.

It was a late night—as paranormal investigations usually are—made even later by daylight saving time and springing ahead. I was sleeping hard when at about 4:00 a.m., I was startled awake by the television turning on. I fumbled for the remote and hit the power button several times. But the television would not turn off. I got out of bed and tried to hit the main power switch, but it still wouldn't turn off. Finally, frustrated (and trying my best not to be scared), I yanked the cord out of the wall, climbed back into bed, and buried my head under my pillow in the hopes of getting a few more hours of sleep. As I drifted off to sleep, I wondered what I was missing. I also tried not to think about the fact that something had gotten past my guides.

When I got home, my left arm was still sore. It had started to feel like someone might have tried to pull it off at the elbow.

As I thought about the pain, I remembered the sketch of the skeleton man. My arm hurt in the same place that it would hurt if someone had twisted my arm behind my back, just as the skeleton man had done in the picture.

I tuned in. I could see the skeleton man. He was really angry. Not just at me—it seemed like he was angry about everything. I wasn't getting any sort of download about what he needed, so I consulted with a friend. I concluded that he wasn't ready to go anywhere yet—he felt like he needed some time to chill out. We worked with his greatest and highest good to try and settle him in a space where he might be able to find some clarity.

I checked back in with him a few days later. This time, a download of information finally came. He was from the late 1920s or early 1930s. He had literally been bullied to death. In his lifetime, all he wanted was to fit in. He was scrawny and little and the likelihood of him fitting in anywhere during that era was not very high. A gang of boys or men had beaten him to death . . . just because. In his afterlife, he was seeking revenge on the living and trying to terrorize them.

It didn't feel to me like he had any connection to the Palmer House during his lifetime, and he didn't feel like he was from anywhere in or near Sauk Centre. It seemed as though he came to the Palmer House by hitching a ride with someone else and had decided to stay when that person left.

Sometimes, people who are sensitive to energy can be susceptible to "attachments" and hitchhiker energies. An attachment is a lower-level soul that quite literally "feeds" off of another person's energy. It's different than a possession in that the entity doesn't enter the person's body. Rather, it hangs out in and near the person's energy field, probably not straying too far, if at all.

After understanding this man's story, I was filled with an immense amount of empathy and understanding. I asked my guides and angels to help him feel unconditional love and acceptance. Together, we wrapped him up in a big ball of love and sent him off to heaven. As he went along on his way, my arm finally felt better.

I wondered if I hadn't let my ego get in the way, maybe he would have been able to find peace a little bit sooner. In that moment, I learned that I can never stop learning when I am doing this work. If I ever start to think I know it all, that's probably when I should retire. But I also acknowledged that the lesson showed up at the right time for me. It was a time when I was ready to learn it.

I learned a lesson about how my ego can get in the way. But it was also a lesson in how everything rises to the surface to be transformed in its own time. Neither myself nor anyone else can rush the universe.

A Bully Cowboy Ghost from Deadwood

In August I was invited to be part of an event at the Palmer House with the paranormal group Things That Go Bump. I had been invited to talk about being an author and was asked to teach a research class on Saturday.

When we went downstairs to check the layout of the basement and decide where we should do the Friday night class, we realized there was a problem.

Employees had reported feeling like there was an aggressive presence in the basement. It was something that went so far as to whack people on the back of the head when they were changing out the soda hookups or getting other supplies.

I was with John and Ryan and they both sensed the aggressive presence in the back corner. Incidentally, it was the same corner the Empath Eater used to occupy, which made me wonder if whatever happened to invade the Palmer House at any given time just looked for the vacant corners.

I couldn't "see" it the way they could, but they could see a dark shape, lumbering back and forth. It seemed to be puffing itself up. I could feel its aggressive nature, but everything about it felt like a pure and simple "bully" presence. It was clear it was just expecting to have the upper hand.

Ryan said, "Hey, we know you're there."

"We won't bother you if you don't bother us," said John. "We don't need or want any trouble from you tonight."

"We will be respectful, and we expect you to be the same," said Ryan.

I felt an instant wave of confusion. This bully was confused that a.) we knew it was there, and b.) none of us were afraid of it. It had never had an interaction with the living world quite like it before.

"He's really confused because we're not afraid of him," I said.

We went back to talking about our setup for the night.

The bully tried again. I could feel it puff itself up. This was confirmed by Ryan and John, who could see him making another attempt to scare us again. I could feel all of his aggression coming at us in full force.

I laughed.

He was such a classic textbook bully, it was hard not to laugh knowing we would never give him the reaction he was expecting. Again, I could feel his complete and utter confusion.

With our laughter, he slunk back into the corner and left us alone, which actually made me feel a little bad for him.

Later, we were talking to one of the waitresses and learned she had spent her summer vacation on a road trip. They had stopped and stayed in the town of Deadwood, South Dakota, which is infamously and notoriously haunted. I got a download of information. The bully had followed her home from Deadwood and had decided that the Palmer House was one heck of a place to hang out.

But hanging out whacking people on the back of the head and trying to scare them every other minute is not behavior that is ever tolerated at the Palmer House—for the living or the dead. I tuned in a few different times to talk to him.

The first time, I tried to explain who I was and what I did. I explained that he didn't have to stay here in this world and could go somewhere where he could enjoy everything he loved about being a cowboy, without the hardship this life had brought him.

He didn't believe me and he wasn't ready. But that was also good for me; it assured me that I wasn't making it up. If I had been making it up, he would have been ready right then and there to ride off into the proverbial sunset.

"I'll be back to check on you again," I told him.

I waited a few days and went back. "You can't stay here," I explained. "You can't keep whacking people on the back of the head; they don't tolerate bullies here. So you can either go back to where you came from, or I can help you go back to Deadwood."

I knew he was listening to me.

"It's got to be getting pretty old. And now that you know people aren't as afraid of you as you thought, I'm sure it's not as much fun either."

I could feel his agreement.

"What was your favorite part about being a cowboy?" I asked him.

I got an image of him on his favorite horse, completely alone, riding along a mountain range with the burning orange and red of a setting sun glowing across the sky. As cliché as that might be, it also happened to be true.

"Well," I said. "Maybe you should go there?"

And suddenly, he was sitting on that same horse, getting ready to ride. Without a word, he tipped his hat, turned his horse, and rode off toward the setting sun.

After that, people stopped getting whacked on the back of the head when they went down to the basement.

"Mr. Boss Man" Moves In

In my work—especially when I am at the Palmer House or Forepaugh's Restaurant—I am often asked why I don't just help *all* of the ghosts cross over. The answer is because that's not my place. I believe that a lot of the ghosts at the Palmer House have chosen to stay for a while, in part to help us learn more about the other side. In my clearing work at the Palmer House, sometimes the ghosts who are supposed to stay there simply go outside and wait until I'm finished. It's funny to see them peering in through the windows from the outside to see if I'm done. That doesn't mean I haven't offered them the opportunity to go if they would like to.

A few years ago, a film crew was working and filming at the Palmer House Hotel. The hotel, pub, and café were all closed to the public for several days so the crew could film. But several people had been asked to come to the hotel to stay there and help out. I was one of the first to arrive, with most everyone else planning to arrive the next day.

When I walked through the front doors, it was very strange to have the building closed to the public. With the hotel closed, there was no need for the regular employees to report to work. It was eerily quiet. The energy in the hotel also felt really agitated—probably because everything was closed and because the film crews had already been in there. There was a collective feeling of confusion: the unregistered guests seemed like they wanted and needed to know what was going on.

In all of the times I'd stayed at the Palmer House Hotel, it was almost always for a big event in which the rooms were nearly all occupied. At events, people stay up until all hours to close down the pub, sometimes even hanging out in the lobby until long after the pub closed. As I sat in the dark, quiet pub catching up with Kelley on a night when it would usually be filled with patrons, it occurred to me for the first time that I would be staying in one of America's most haunted hotels almost completely by myself. It was even more intimidating knowing that the ghosts in the hotel were feeling agitated and worked up because of the filming that had taken place the night before. I will never forget the moment that Kelley turned to me and asked me to follow her to the back door and lock it behind her.

But I heard Annette's voice telling me to "pull on my big girl pants," so I wrapped my head around my solitude and followed Kelley to the back door. Locking it behind her, I made my way back through the vacant kitchen, turning lights off as I found them along my way.

I climbed the dark stairs, found my way down the hallway in the dark using the flashlight on my phone, and let myself into my room. As soon as I had the door safely locked behind me, I grabbed my crystals and asked my guides to help me lock my room in an energy grid. I asked them to keep the ghosts away so I could sleep. Three of my guides stood guard at my bed, and I'm pretty sure Mac stood guard at the doorway.

At 3:30 a.m., I was startled awake. Not because of a noise or a light turning on (both have been known to happen there regularly), but because I felt like there was a mob of ghosts out in the hallway. I heard someone asking if "the story lady" would come out and explain. They wanted answers to their questions about the film crews—they wanted to know what was going on and why the regular employees were gone.

In my half-awake state, I visualized myself going out in the hallway to talk to them. I stood at a podium that suddenly appeared out of nowhere and spoke into a microphone that also magically appeared. "If you don't like it, you don't have to stay," I explained. "You have freewill choice. Anyone who needs help leaving, I am happy to help you cross over." With that, they all slunk away to whatever corners they'd come from and I was left standing alone.

But every now and then, a ghost will show up at the Palmer House who isn't supposed to be there. Sometimes those ghosts are looking for help and they usually find it pretty quickly. The unregistered guests can stay until they are ready to go as long as they play by the rules. For example, they are not allowed to whack people upside the head or push anyone around. There have been a few times where those ghosts aren't necessarily ready to cross over, but they aren't cooperating either, so they have to leave. Those situations can get a little tricky, and often require some creativity.

In October, I kept getting warning flashes that someone was going to try to bring a Ouija board into the Palmer House. The flashes became strong and recurrent enough that I felt like I needed to warn Kelley to be on the lookout. One day, she called and told me the housekeepers had found the instructions that came with a Ouija board underneath a bed. It had obviously fallen out of a game recently, after someone had snuck it in.

Ouija boards are forbidden at the Palmer House—and for good reason. There's enough stuff going on there; it doesn't need any extra drama. In my opinion, intent is everything when dealing with the paranormal, and the entire intent of a

Ouija board is to open up a doorway to the other side. They seem harmless enough at first glance (there is even a version that is sold in the toy aisle with board games like Monopoly). The problem with Ouija boards, in my opinion, is that it's impossible to know who or what is going to come in. I've heard stories about mischievous spirits who pretend to be the loved ones that participants are trying to contact.

Another problem with Ouija boards is that most often, those who use them don't know how to close them down properly. Therefore, the doorway they've opened stays open, letting things pass from that world to this one quite freely, like a portable portal.

I once heard a long-time paranormal researcher speaking at a convention explain that he often got phone calls in the middle of the night from teenagers who thought it would be fun to play with a Ouija board. They would open up the session (and the doorway to the other side), get scared, and throw the board across the room, therefore leaving the doorway open.

Another issue with the Ouija board is the reputation the Ouija board has obtained within the collective consciousness. When we put thoughts or ideas out there into the universe, that thought or idea becomes a strand of energy. That strand of energy combines with the energy strands from others to wind together and create a collective thought, or consciousness. With respect to Ouija boards, the tool in and of itself isn't necessarily dangerous. But because so many people have declared them as "bad" or "evil," that's exactly what they have become. Many people have judged them as "bad," therefore, the collective consciousness of the Ouija board has a darker, more evil personality than it might have otherwise had. It's a good reminder to be careful with our judgment and condemnation, and also to make sure that we are only putting positive thoughts out into the universe.

In this particular case, after the instruction manual for the Ouija board was found, the office began to feel a little crowded. Kelley mentioned feeling like someone was watching her work. The energy felt off. At one point, a disembodied voice actually yelled, "Get out." And it was loud enough to hear.

When I tuned in to the situation, my crew showed me a character from a Disney Pixar movie. I laughed. I'm sure they showed me a cartoon character because that instantly makes the scenario comical and less threatening. It's hard to be afraid of something I was comparing to a movie I watched with my children when they were preschoolers.

This ghost was large and overweight, and he was wearing a suit. He was on the phone constantly. He was trying to move himself into the offices and apartment of the Palmer House Hotel in Sauk Centre, Minnesota. My crew told me that he had come in through the open door the Ouija board had provided. He liked the location so much he decided to stay . . . and take it over.

He was older, and he had two helpers with him. My guides actually referred to them as "minions." Their only purpose seemed to be to answer their boss's every beck and call. One was a woman, tall and skinny, with her blond hair in a bun. She was an assistant of sorts. The other, a man, was small and wiry, with thin glasses. He seemed to me to be the "numbers" guy, whatever that meant in this situation. Their motives were very clear: they were locked in a servitude of sorts to help their boss with whatever he needed or wanted. And what he wanted was to move into the Palmer House Hotel.

However, when Mr. Boss Man made the decision to move into his new office, he had no idea how quickly the real staff and employees of the Palmer House Hotel would notice he was there. He also never could have anticipated that they would actually have the ability to do anything about his presence.

He very clearly had a mob-boss mentality. He was specifically looking for a space to take over his "operation." He liked the office, but he also really enjoyed the quiet of the empty room next door to the office. At one time, this part of the hotel had been a live-in apartment for a family that lived in the hotel while they ran it. Eventually, the kitchen and living area were turned into the office and conference room. The bedrooms and bathrooms from this space are still referred to as "the apartment" and are not part of the regular hotel room rotation.

What exactly this "operation" involved was anyone's guess. In any event, it became pretty clear pretty quickly that someone like me would not be able to have a nice conversation that would convince this guy to move out and be on his way. He wasn't going to take direction or advice from anyone, especially a soccer mom like me.

But my guides started showing me ideas of things that would make the place much less "comfortable" and might even encourage him to leave. For example, they told me he had an aversion to certain colors ... specifically pastel pink and purple. He also hated the smell of lavender because it reminded him of his mother. He didn't want to think about his mother when he was working on his "operation."

In fact, they suggested that if he thought too much about his mother, he would feel guilty and not even want to stay there. I passed this information along. Kelley purchased the most obnoxious bouquet of pink flowers and fresh lavender she could find and put it in the middle of the apartment. She also found pastel quilts for the bed from the laundry shelves. I concentrated on the energy of the space and tried to tune it to a frequency he would find uncomfortable—which wasn't hard since we'd already been working on raising the vibration in that space. We waited a few days to check in again. I could feel his agitation. My crew suggested sending some limousines to pick him up.

I wasn't exactly sure how to order up limos for members of the netherworld. My crew assured me they had it covered and three limos would arrive the following day. They wanted there to be three—one for each spirit—because the minions were probably tired of their servitude. Mr. Boss Man wasn't necessarily ready to cross over, but there was a chance the minions might be.

The three limos arrived at the door the very next day. My guess is that the two minions probably sent their cars to the light. I have no idea where Mr. Boss Man ended up ... he is probably still driving around in his, thinking he is running the underworld.

But at least he's not sitting in the offices at the Palmer House Hotel.

In hindsight, looking back at this particular story, I learned something about my guides. They bring me information in the way that makes the most sense for me to be able to handle it and in a way I can analyze appropriately. Was there really a character right out of a Disney movie trying to invade the Palmer House? No, probably not. But I have no doubt that something was there. There was tangible evidence in the form of a disembodied voice telling the real owners to "get out."

I also know that the atmosphere shifted after the work was done. I believe that my guides were not only giving me the information in a way that made it easy for me to figure out what was going on, but also in an incredibly nonthreatening manner. Even the fact that they described the two helpers as "minions" helped me handle the situation efficiently and without fear.

I am grateful to my entire team of spirit guide helpers. Without them, I would not be able to do this work. I have the gifts to see, feel, know, and understand them, but they are the ones who actually show and tell me what to do with what I see, feel, know, and understand.

SEVEN
OTHER REALMS
AND DIMENSIONS

Our Ghost Stories Ink group had the unique opportunity to investigate one of the most notoriously haunted historic properties in St. Paul—Forepaugh's Restaurant. Forepaugh's has an interesting history. Situated in the Irving Park neighborhood next to the park and across from the former home of one of Minnesota's first governors, it sits in the heart of what was once St. Paul's earliest, most affluent neighborhood.

This majestic neighborhood faded into disrepair as the wealthy eventually chose homes up the hill and moved to the more desirable Summit Avenue addresses. It was saved from demolition in the 1970s after serving as a boarding house and apartment building for many years. The new owners had a vision and reinvented the space as Forepaugh's Restaurant.

For more than forty years, it was a favorite fine-dining destination for many. With such an intriguing whispered past, it made a celebratory graduation dinner or special anniversary date that much more exciting. Forepaugh's has since closed its doors, but this amazing building will be back in some way, shape, or form. It's a special place that seems to know how to take care of itself.

The first time I ever set foot in the building was for my law school graduation dinner. It was before I knew anything about my own gifts, or even understood anything about ghosts. But I had heard it was haunted. I fully admit to looking over my shoulder the entire evening, hoping to catch a glimpse of a strange mist or shadowy apparition.

Legend tells the story of a maid named Molly. She had an affair with the master of the house, Joseph Forepaugh, and became pregnant with his baby. When Joseph's angry wife insisted the relationship end, rumor has it that Molly committed suicide by hanging herself from a light fixture on the third floor. Not long after, Joseph was found near the train tracks with a bullet in his head and a pistol in his hand. It's a storyline worthy of a made-for-television movie adaptation.

Both Molly and Joseph have been rumored to haunt the house ever since. Diners and staff can attest to many paranormal experiences witnessed with their own eyes throughout the years. And yet, paranormal activity is not something the owners and managers have always been ready to admit.

My group, Ghost Stories Ink, was invited to investigate the restaurant. The managers wanted our group to investigate on our own and then present our findings. They would even create a special menu and make it into a special event dinner. As the historian and researcher for GSI, I couldn't have been more excited. A lot was known about the house in its early days, while next to nothing was known about it during the time it served as a boarding house.

I dove into the research and spent hours with dusty old books in the basements of the Landmark Center and the Minnesota Historical Society Library. Armed with extensive research—which included lists of names of previous apartment residents—we investigated the house in April. We even had a local news team there to cover the investigation.

Prior to our investigation, I took a few precautionary measures. I knew that this particular neighborhood had some heavier energy. I did not want to turn on a lighthouse of sorts for any passing spirits. I locked in the house with an energy of protection and an energy of invisibility and asked that only those energies who had a connection to the house in some way be allowed to participate in our investigation. For our purposes, it was important that the ghosts and energies we interacted with were ones whose stories were relevant to the house.

Over the course of the evening, we had lots of paranormal activity. At one point, I was interviewed by the news team who was covering the investigation. This interview actually turned out to include paranormal evidence. The cameraman's light slid down off its setting without warning, shocking everyone in the room while we were filming. We also had an amazing EVP and flashlight session in the back servant stairwell that helped to clarify and correct some of the old rumors.

Molly really wanted everyone to know that she didn't kill herself in what is now a dining room. She was embarrassed and ashamed. She wouldn't have done anything to bring any further attention to herself. Instead, she died in the back servants' stairway. When we walked up this staircase from the main floor, we could actually feel the heaviness descend as we approached the third floor. When I stood on the landing on the second floor and closed my eyes, I could see her body hanging there from the top railing.

We also realized that a lot of the paranormal activity on the third floor actually had a different culprit. A man named George lived in one of the third-floor apartments for over a decade at the end of his life. He was a veteran of both World War I and World War II. We captured an SLS image of an energy we think was George in the back dining room on the third floor.

An SLS camera will map in a stick figure when it detects something that might be a ghost. Like a lot of ghost-hunting gadgets, an SLS camera was adapted from video game technology that lets users play without having to hold a controller. Gamers using this technology had found that sometimes when they would leave the room for something, upon their return it looked as though something had started playing their game. Equipment specialists realized that the camera was picking up the same body points of a ghost as it would for someone playing the video game.

In this case, I felt something hit me in the bum three times and I said so out loud. From across the room, Kevin, who was filming, started to laugh. It turned out that just before I mentioned anything, an image had mapped in behind me and kicked me in the bum three times. To this day, it remains one of the best SLS images we've ever captured.

One beautiful morning after our investigation, George showed up for me. He was ready to cross over, but he wanted me to pass along a message to the managers at Forepaugh's.

"Please tell them I'm coming right back," he said. "I'm coming back to help keep an eye on things from the other side."

"Okay," I assured him. "I will let them know."

In July we went back and presented all of our evidence at a special dinner. While there, one of our attendees asked the question, "Why does Molly choose to stay? Why does she want to be here?"

In my head—as if she were answering the question herself—I heard very clearly, "Why wouldn't I stay? I broke every single commandment there ever was. Why on earth would I want to go on to whatever is next?"

I wasn't quite ready to admit to anyone else in that room that I heard Molly answer that question for herself. So out loud I explained, "Molly was most likely an Irish immigrant, which means she was probably Catholic. Catholics believe in heaven and hell, and breaking any of the ten commandments certainly shortens your odds at getting into heaven. I'm sure she probably didn't want to take that chance."

Our guest was satisfied with my answer, as was Molly.

But a few weeks before we went back to give our presentation, one of the managers reported that he felt an uncomfortable presence in the basement. It was something dark and creepy that was bothering the employees.

———

The basement at Forepaugh's Restaurant is the energy center of the house—it houses the kitchen. When the manager mentioned that he was feeling something down there that he knew didn't belong, I got a download of information, but I didn't necessarily trust it right away.

I knew from that inner place of knowing that what he was talking about had never been human. It wasn't as bad as the entity that had been at the Palmer House, but it was definitely a non-human entity. Not wanting to alarm him and not entirely sure what to do about it, I told him I would check in remotely when I got home and get back to him.

Intrigued, I tuned in as soon as I had the chance—but I didn't really believe what I was getting. The information that I got was that this was a fairy. And not just any fairy, but a dark, fallen fairy. I had no frame of reference for fairies.

So I sent a note to a friend who I knew wouldn't think I was crazy. It was something along the lines of, "I think my client has a dark fairy in their basement. Is that even possible?" It was one of the stranger text messages I've ever sent.

She answered, "Yes." And then she pulled in a mutual friend who would know what to do about it.

Meanwhile, I got another download of information. This fairy had come in with the very first paranormal group that had been allowed to investigate the house. It had become fascinated by the kitchen. There was a great deal of energy radiating from the kitchen, which was underneath the surface of the earth, and this entity decided it wanted to stay.

That night I had an incredibly vivid dream. I could see the fairy. His black wings were tattered and torn, and he was so sad.

He actually looked more like a moth-man creature than what I would have imagined a fairy to look like. While he'd become fascinated by the energy in the basement, he had recently realized he was trapped.

"Can you please just open the door and let me out?" he asked me in my dream. He had the same sad face my youngest child would give me when she really wanted something but knew I was going to say no.

I didn't entirely trust that I could just "let him out"—the whole concept of simply opening the door and "letting him out" felt entirely wrong. It also felt like maybe I wasn't getting the full story.

"I'm not sure," I told him in my dream. "Let me check on a few things and I'll get back to you."

I mean, really. I was not about to just trust whatever a fallen fairy was telling me. I hadn't believed they even existed until a few days before. And presumably, a dark fairy wouldn't be quite as trustworthy as any other kind of fairy.

But at the moment, I had another, bigger problem. I had to tell the managers at the restaurant about it. I couldn't go forward with any work to clear him out without first getting their approval and consent.

I imagined the conversation in my head. *Hi, I just wanted to tell you that you have a dark, fallen fairy in your basement and he wants me to open the door and let him out. Is that cool with you?*

In my imaginary conversation, both managers looked at me like I was certifiably nuts and then burst out laughing. They would have been right to laugh. I would have laughed if someone were telling *me* that news.

But at the same time, everything about this information felt the same as always. Even though the information was completely unbelievable at face value, it was also coming from my guides in the same way it always did. They had never steered me wrong before. I didn't have any reason to believe they would start messing with me now. I decided to trust them and believe the information download I was getting—despite the fact that it seemed fantastic and from an unfamiliar world.

I took a deep breath and gathered my courage. Instead of talking to the managers in person, I sent an email that went something along the lines of, "Do you mind if I work on clearing something that I picked up on in the kitchen? I think it's the thing that is making everyone uncomfortable, and I think I know what to do about it. I can do it from home; I don't even have to come in. But most of all, I can assure you, it's something that is not supposed to be there."

I got the response that I could go ahead.

I figured by postponing the reveal on what "it" was, I could clear it out. If the kitchen felt better when I was done, maybe they'd be more inclined to believe me.

I tuned in to the fairy and got another download of information. He'd made a few bad choices in his fairy life and gotten caught up in a darkness he hadn't fully anticipated. He had disappeared from his dark realm and when he became trapped in the kitchen, he had been written off by the rest of his dark fairy cronies as MIA. He wasn't expected back anywhere and it was actually the perfect opportunity for him to escape the bad choices he had made.

I called on my Beetle Man guide knowing that he would offer insight, expertise, and authority. All of my guides agreed that I could let him out if he agreed to go on to whatever his next highest level was supposed to be and accepted my help and assistance to do so.

I presented all of this to the dark fairy creature. The whole time I was talking, he was staring at my Beetle Man standing next to me. When I was finished explaining the terms and conditions, he agreed. I became very aware that the presence of my Beetle Man standing next to me somehow gave me authority I might not have otherwise had. I wrapped up my new fairy friend in a bubble and sent him on his way.

After, I was overwhelmed with a feeling of relief. My dark fairy friend was relieved that he was free to start again with no one from his previously dark world being any the wiser.

The next challenge I faced was to come clean with the managers of Forepaugh's and explain to them what had been haunting their kitchen. It wasn't long before I found an opportunity to talk to both of them together.

"I should probably tell you what was in the basement."

They both looked at me expectantly.

"This is going to sound a little crazy, but I think it was a dark fairy. He came in with the first paranormal group and was fascinated by the underground energy of the kitchen. However, when I set the parameters for our investigation, I accidentally locked him in the house and he couldn't get out. That's why he felt so persistent about leaving with you at the end of the night when you were ready to go home. He wanted someone to let him out."

They stared, eyebrows raised.

"He's gone now," I said. "He realized he'd made some bad choices and was ready to start fresh, so I sent him on his way."

"Well, that's good," said one.

"It feels better down there," said the other.

Avery's New Guide

My kids are sensitive to energy. One of my goals in everything I do is to try to teach them better than I was taught. When I was the same age, I would see dark shadows in my room and feel like someone was watching me. When I reported it to anyone, I was told over and over that it was "just my imagination" and "there's no such thing as ghosts."

I don't say that to my kids. When I started writing books about ghosts, I knew I'd need a better way to explain it to them. I would never be able to get away with telling them that there was no such thing when it was the very thing I was writing stories about.

I also obviously know better now. There *is* such a thing as ghosts. I've seen enough paranormal evidence. When we are on an investigation and we ask a ghost that we are interacting with to finish a knock pattern on a wall—and it does, or when we get an EVP of a ghost saying its name when we ask, it's enough proof for me. With my psychic work, my logical brain is satisfied with the validation my guides help provide.

But I also know that what's out there on the other side—whatever is trying to interact with us—it's not usually something that anyone needs to be afraid of. It's energy. And when it's intelligent energy, it's usually just trying to let us know that it's there. And in some cases, it's also asking for help. The less fear we put out there into the world, the better it is for everyone.

Instead of telling my kids that ghosts don't exist, I talk to them about bubbling their own space and keeping their energy fields safe, especially at night and in places with large crowds. In my experience, empathic children are much more likely to pick up the bad moods and negative energy from other people than any sort of ghost energy that might be out there. A bubble of protection helps protect against all of that emotion and keeps them from taking on the angry emotions of others as their own. It also doesn't hurt to be overprepared.

I try to teach my children that they are in charge of their own energy fields. It's their responsibility to keep their energy fields safe. As the humans with the real bodies, our energy is infinitely stronger than anything else that might be out there.

My kids carry rocks and crystals around everywhere. Some crystals are known to have protective qualities. When I pick up school clothes to throw them in the washer and they are heavier than they should be (and make a loud clunk when I toss them in the washer), I know I need to dig them back out again to retrieve the chunk of rose quartz, crystal quartz, or amethyst.

I don't worry too much about what the experts or books "say" a crystal is supposed to do. Instead, I let my kids pick out the rocks and crystals that resonate for them. Rocks and crystals carry energy that can facilitate and encourage different vibrations. Every person is different, and therefore could need different rocks. For example, amethyst is actually a grounding rock for me. However, I have yet to find a crystal book that would identify amethyst as a grounding rock. Usually, it's identified as a rock that raises a person's vibration to bring them up to a higher level.

My kids also use Florida Water in their rooms to reset their space. Florida Water is a metaphysical spray and it's actually not water from Florida, it's a shamanic spray from Peru. It comes in a tall, thin bottle that we put in a spray bottle and cut with water. It will instantly settle nerves, clear nausea and headaches caused by shifting EMF energies, and generally make them feel better. It has improved their bad moods, focused their attention during homework, and—most importantly—empowered them to control their space. They've even been known to pack it in their bags when they head to an overnight at Grandma's or a friend's house.

Over the winter holiday break, my oldest son (then age fourteen) asked me to scan his room because he felt like something was there. I scanned his room and told him everything was fine. A day later, he asked me to do it again. Again, I scanned his space but again, I didn't get anything. I told him there was nothing to worry about.

This went on for three days. Finally, he came into my room late one night and sat down on my bed.

"Mom, I really feel like there's something in my room you need to clear." His room is on the third floor of our house—he has the half-story attic that we converted into his space. It's a perfect place for a teenager to get away from his younger brother and sister.

I tuned in one more time, scanned, and didn't get any sort of lost spirit/ghostly type energy. "Maybe it's Grandpa," I said. But my gut answered right away, *Nope, it's not Grandpa.*

"It's not Grandpa, Mom," he said. "I know what Grandpa feels like."

I sighed. I had been flipping through a new deck of sacred geometry mandalas and had a thought. "Maybe we should pull a card and ask?"

He shrugged.

I shuffled my deck and carefully selected a card. The message was something along the lines of, "Be open to the possibilities of other dimensions."

"Shit," I said, instantly understanding what was in his room and realizing what had happened. I hadn't picked up on anything because I'd been scanning for human energies, not inner-earth energies.

"What?" he asked.

"Give me a minute and I'll let you know."

"Okay, fine. But I'm going downstairs to wait. I'm not going back up there until you're done."

"Fair enough," I said, feeling bad the kid had been sleeping up there alone for the last three nights.

I grabbed my own rocks. When I am working to clear a space or better tune in to energies, I hold a crystal quartz in my right hand and a chunk of rough amethyst in my left to both raise my vibration while staying grounded to the earth's energy. I tuned in again to his room.

This time, I could see a little gargoyle-type gnome creature sitting on his weight bench. The image came with a story download. The previous summer, my boys had made regular trips to the river on their bikes. We live in an urban area, but we are only about two miles away from the shores of the Mississippi River. It offers two adventurous boys the perfect opportunity to escape into nature despite their location. On New Year's Eve—a frigid Minnesota day—our whole family had gone bowling at a bar in Minneapolis, just on the other side of the river. Somehow, some way, this little guy had recognized Avery when we were driving back across the river and followed him home.

He really liked Avery and wanted to keep him safe. He'd been sleeping in his room ever since. But he also seemed like he was a lower vibration, almost like a ghost of whatever creature he had been. My guides told me he needed to cross over. In my experience thus far, it almost seems easier to cross other dimensional beings. They don't seem to have the same constraints that our human freewill choice sometimes adds to the mix. It doesn't seem like I have to convince them to go in the same way I have to convince ghosts. I've wondered if maybe this is because they took a wrong turn and ended up in the wrong realm.

As always, I trusted the advice from my crew, wrapped him up in a bubble, and sent him on his way so he could go where he was supposed to go and transform into whatever his next highest version was meant to be.

But I had a bigger challenge still to come. I needed to figure out how to explain to my son that an inner-earth troll-gargoyle-gnome thing had followed him home and into our house. I called him back upstairs and together we went up to his room.

"Okay," I said. "This is going to sound a little weird."

He narrowed his eyes at me. My kids know that if something sounds weird to their mother, it's actually going to be more than a *little* weird. Most likely, it'll be insanely freaky.

"You know that nothing can get into our house that isn't light or love, right?"

He nodded.

"Okay, good. Nothing can get into our house that isn't light or love. This is something that followed you home because he liked you. He wanted to keep you safe."

My son stared harder at me. "What was it?"

"Well..." I said, searching for the right words. "That's a little hard to explain."

"Try," he said.

"Okay." I took a deep breath. "It felt like it was from an inner-earth realm, like the fairies, but this wasn't a fairy. This was more of a gnome-type thing and looked a little like one of the creatures from a Star Wars movie."

"Which one?" He asked, his face stoic.

"It was a little like the guard-type guys from Jabba the Hutt's palace in *Return of the Jedi*."

His eyes got wide.

"But cuter," I added quickly. "He just really liked you and wanted to keep you safe."

"I know," he said. "It slept right there for the last three nights." He pointed at his weight bench.

"Really?" I asked. "You've got to admit that's kind of cool."

He shrugged.

"It's gone now, right?" I asked.

"Shouldn't you know that?" he asked.

"I think it is," I said quickly. "But it doesn't hurt to have you sense and feel that it is too, considering you're the one who knew it was sleeping on your weight bench for the last few days. And I couldn't even pick up on it when I scanned your room."

He looked carefully around his room. "Yeah, it's gone."

"Okay, good." I went back downstairs to my cards.

A few minutes later, I got a nudge. I tuned back in. The inner-earth creature was back, only this time it was a higher vibration. Now that he was a higher vibration, he seemed a lot cuter than he had before. The cute little guy sat on the edge of my bed, swinging his feet. I knew, without knowing how I knew, that he wanted to be a guide for Avery.

This was weird, even for me. This one needed confirmation. I went downstairs and found my pendulum and ran through a series of questions. I was right. And somehow, I knew I never in a million years could have invented this scenario if I'd tried— even with my crazy imagination. Sometimes, that logic serves really well as a way to validate the crazy in my head.

I sighed. But now I had to go back up and tell my son.

"I've got something else to tell you," I said, climbing the steps up to the attic.

He looked up from his book. "What?" The stoic tone and narrowed eyes were back.

"It's already back."

He didn't say anything.

"It came back because it really, really likes you. And in its next phase, it chose to be a guide for you. So it's back, but it's at a higher vibration and now its purpose is to act as a guide and protector for you. It will be there for you, if you need it. You just have to ask it for help if you do."

He was quiet, obviously processing the information I'd just shared.

"That's pretty cool, isn't it?" I finally asked.

"Yeah," he agreed. "That's pretty cool."

EIGHT
PORTALS AND WANDERERS

We were back at Forepaugh's for another investigation, this time with a different team of investigators, and my friend Nicole was part of the group. We had a goal for our investigation. We wanted to try to confirm any psychic impressions with whatever paranormal evidence we could gather.

We split into two groups. After a while, I was down in the parlor (my favorite room at Forepaugh's) and we were using a spirit box. A spirit box is a piece of equipment that scans the radio waves, with the idea that a ghostly energy can harness the scanning radio frequencies to use the spirit box to say words and sentences.

A call came through on the walkie-talkie that there was something happening in the office and one of the managers had asked if I would come up. There was a full-length, free-standing mirror that had been pushed up against the exterior back wall of the office. This mirror used to serve as the doorway to the office, blocking it off from the patrons and staff. But recently, a waitress had tripped over the heavy foot of the mirror, spilling an entire tray of food. To be safe and not risk repeating the same mistake, the mirror had been moved out of the way and shoved against the back wall.

There is an old wives' tale that mirrors against exterior walls can serve as portals—or gateways—to other realms and dimensions. In this case, the group had captured extensive SLS images of figures coming out of the mirror and going back in.

The SLS camera had mapped in several different stick figures coming and going from the mirror. The activity was repetitive and frequent, and the vibe didn't feel happy or playful—it felt as if whatever was popping in and out of the mirror was up to no good.

The decision had been made to shut it down. Nicole explained that she was going to go through a process her guides had showed her to bind the mirror. I wasn't entirely sure what I was going to do, but I felt compelled to go stand next to the mirror.

As Nicole began to work, I felt a rush of energy that wanted to quickly enter the office through the mirror before she could get it shut down. I focused all of my energy and attention on holding off these entities and trying to keep them at bay.

Kevin kept the SLS camera pointed on the mirror as we worked. As we began to work, the paranormal activity came to a halt. The SLS images quieted and nothing else came through the mirror.

Another Portal Mirror

Even though our first trip to Florida resulted in a ghost stealing my jewelry, we returned to the very same house the following year for spring break. I figured that since I'd already helped the ghost who had been haunting it the last time, we might as well go back. I also had a sliver of hope that if we went back to the same house, maybe the ghost I had helped would be able to figure out how to get my jewelry back to me again. This time, though, I packed my sage and a few crystals . . . just in case.

It was a good thing, too. The first night we were there, I woke up in the middle of the night. There were a lot of strange tapping sounds and noises coming from the kitchen.

With a groan, I rolled my eyes. "Seriously?" I asked my guides. "There's another one? But I'm on vacation."

They reminded me that it didn't matter.

In my mind's eye, I scanned the other rooms in the house. There was a skinny, younger man with scraggly hair—a ghost— standing in the kitchen. He beckoned for me to follow him out to the front yard. My body stayed in bed, but in my mind's eye I walked out to the front lawn.

When I walked out the front door, I saw a large gathering of ghosts waiting in front of the house on the lawn. He'd been elected to come in to get me.

"The bus will be here in a minute," I told them all. And sure enough, a big yellow school bus showed up. Slowly, they all got on it. But there were many more ghosts than there were spots on the bus. So the bus started to grow and grow until it was long enough to make room for everyone that needed to get on it. Apparently, buses destined to go to heaven can do that.

It took me a long time to go back to sleep after that. As I lay there, my guides told me to look for a mirror portal the next day. In the morning my husband asked, "What was going on last night? Why couldn't you sleep?"

"A lot of reasons," I said. "But a big one is because of all of the ghosts. There were a bunch waiting out in the front yard last night for me to help them. But don't worry, I called in a bus so they could get to heaven. They aren't there anymore."

He promptly changed the subject.

Not long after, everyone was out of the house. I got out my sage, lit it, and walked through all the bedrooms. As I did, I looked for a mirror that could be a portal. There weren't any mirrors hanging on exterior walls, so I chalked up the existence of a mirror portal to my imagination. I assumed that I had been projecting its existence. After all, the paranormal investigation at Forepaugh's that had revealed a portal mirror had taken place only a few weeks before we left for vacation, so I must've just had mirrors on my mind.

I came out of the room the kids were using and walked straight into my mother-in-law.

"Oh," I said, startled. "I'm uh … just doing a little smudging. There were a bunch of ghosts that needed some help last night."

I realized something about myself in that moment. I really, truly, no longer cared what anyone thought of me for the work that I do. I am just me, trying to be the best me I can be.

"That's very interesting," she said. And I knew she meant it.

———

As we were packing up to leave, I was going through the house looking for anything we might have left behind. As I pulled the door to the kids' bathroom to check the hooks behind it for any stray swimsuits or towels, my mouth dropped open in surprise. There, behind the door, was a giant, full-length mirror that ran the length of the wall. And . . . it was against an exterior wall.

"So I guess there really is a portal mirror?" I asked one of my guides.

He just rolled his eyes. "I tried to tell you!"

I called in another guide to help me close it down. Together we worked. He showed me how to wrap various layers of energy around it to bind it and close off the gateway to other dimensions.

We packed up our things and went on our way. I was a little disappointed that I still didn't have my travel bag of jewelry back. I don't know how or if I will ever get that jewelry back, but I haven't given up hope that I will see it again someday.

A Tag-Along

During the week of the Fourth of July, we had the chance to visit my in-laws at a lake in northern Minnesota. We spent time on the lake; the boys went fishing; we sat in the sun and swam in the water. It was a perfect week at the lake in Minnesota.

One night, we went out to dinner. All of us piled into a van and we were on our way. On the way home, Avery (my oldest) turned to me and said, "Mom, let's play Haunted or Not Haunted." Haunted or Not Haunted is a game my boys invented where they point to a house and I have to say if it's haunted or not haunted.

"You play," I said. "I'll listen." I'd had two glasses of wine at dinner and didn't think I should be doing any sort of haunted games at the moment. But somehow, the conversation shifted quickly into something else.

The next day, Avery and I took the kayaks out to paddle along the lakeshore to see some of the other cabins. As we paddled along in the sunshine, I noticed an interesting cabin. It was old, small, and in disrepair. It didn't have a dock. It made me wonder if one of the other cabins on either side of it might be using it as a bunkhouse or a kids' cabin. If I were a kid, I wouldn't want to have to stay in it.

"Avery," I called out.

He turned to look at me from his kayak.

"Are we still playing Haunted or Not Haunted?" I asked, pointing at the run-down building.

"Yeah," he said. "I'd say that one looks pretty haunted." He stopped talking for a minute. "It feels pretty haunted too."

An hour later, I was sitting on the shore with my mother-in-law, her significant other, and the neighbors. Everyone started talking about the other cabins on the lake and some of the local scandals.

"What about the run-down one just a few down from here?" I asked. "The one without a dock?"

"Oh," said the neighbor, "that's owned by a woman from California. She only comes once every few years. Her father passed away and she refuses to sell it. She's sentimental about it."

"That's interesting," I said. And more than explained why it felt haunted.

A few nights after we'd gotten home, I was in a deep sleep. Next to me, my husband flew out of bed and I heard him go upstairs to where our oldest was sleeping.

When he came back, even though I was still half asleep, I asked, "What's wrong?"

"I heard a thump coming from upstairs."

As he said it, I heard the same thump. But I was in such a deep sleep that even though I was comprehending his words, it was like my body couldn't wake up enough to have any emotion about it.

I rolled over and promptly fell back to sleep, not giving it another thought—until a few hours later. At 3:00 a.m., I woke with a start. A huge thump sounded from the room just above. It was like footsteps, but there was only one foot. It was almost like someone intentionally dropped something heavy on the floor right above our heads. This time, my husband slept through it.

I went up to check for myself, but my son was sleeping hard. I looked around his room. Nothing had fallen off his bed. There was nothing that could have made the thumping sound.

I went back downstairs, got back into bed, and heard it again.

Remembering the time the gnome had followed my oldest son home and I hadn't done anything about it, I made myself get back up and go downstairs to look for my rocks. I had a hunch I knew who it was.

Finding a quiet spot in the office at 3:30 in the morning, I sat in the corner chair and tuned in.

I could see the old man from the abandoned lake house. Knowing that if something had followed us home and was in my house, it was ready to go, I wrapped him up in a bubble without a fuss and sent him on his way.

My husband didn't ask about it the following morning and I didn't volunteer anything.

An Unexpected Helper in Ely

Not long ago, we went away for a family weekend in northern Minnesota. We visited and stayed in the town of Ely. I hadn't been there in years, certainly not since I knew I was psychic. As we drove into town, I felt an overwhelming feeling of heaviness that came on suddenly and then disappeared. It made me think that surely, I'd be woken up in the middle of the night by someone needing help.

But when I woke up at 8:00 a.m., morning had arrived and I'd been allowed to sleep through the night. Shortly after I woke up, my middle son, Luke, wandered into our room. He had been sleeping on a pull-out futon in the living room, just outside our room, next to the front door of the motel room suite.

"I woke up in the middle of the night," he said. "And there was a dead guy standing over me. He was looking at me and watching me sleep."

"What did you do?" I asked him, worried.

"I made sure my bubble was locked up tight. And then I wrapped him up in a bubble and asked that the bubble take him to heaven. And then I went back to sleep."

It took me a minute to find my words. There were a lot of thoughts going through my head all at once. But mostly, I was so surprised and proud of him.

"That's great," I finally said.

He just shrugged and went off to brush his teeth.

I wish someone had taught me how to do that when I was thirteen. My life would have been a lot easier.

NINE
CONFUSION AND CHAOS

Not long ago, Kevin, Jessica and I were back at Forepaugh's. As we walked through the whole house, we found ourselves in the basement kitchen. As I stood in the small space, I was suddenly caught in a wave of chaotic energy that made me want to pace back and forth, throwing my hands up in the air.

"Why do I feel like I want to do this when I stand here?" I asked the managers, Mimi and Joe, as I walked back and forth throwing my hands up in the air.

"That's exactly what the prep cook who works there does too. All day long," Mimi said.

"It's more than that," I said, closing my eyes to see the image better.

I could see a woman. She was from the late 1800s; I could tell by her Victorian style. She was wearing a purple dress. The skirt was long and full and the shoulders of her sleeves were slightly puffy. She also wore a broach pinned just under the collar, at her throat.

"It's a woman," I said, and I stopped to tune in to the lower-vibrational energy. "There's a woman here, and she doesn't know that she's dead."

The story dropped in. She had been frantically going about her day, in a rush to do all of her shopping and errands. She had been crossing West Seventh when she'd been hit by a horse-drawn carriage or wagon of some type. She had been trampled and killed. Her ghostly energy got right back up and went back about her busy day. She didn't even know that she was dead; she had just continued on with her chaotic energy. It seemed like it would be that way for eternity. She had been living more than a hundred years of her afterlife stuck in her frantic day. Somehow, she had found her way to the basement of Forepaugh's and was haunting one particular corner of the kitchen. She thrived on the hectic energy of the cooking staff as they went about a busy night. It somehow made her feel at home.

"I can understand why the cook who works here always throws his hands up and down and paces back and forth," I said.

I told them about the poor woman who was stuck.

Her messy bun was tilted to one side and her eyes darted back and forth as I began to try to talk to her.

"Stop," I said. "Look at me."

But she was so "busy" she wouldn't stop to listen. It was almost like I had to tune a radio dial to adjust her frequency, but instead of adjusting the station, I felt like I was slowing her down. She was moving in slow motion.

Her eyes darted, and finally they fixed on me. Her empty gaze locked in on mine. I realized there wasn't really an easy way to tell a ghost that they were dead.

"You are stuck in the day that you died. You can be done now. You get to go somewhere different."

Her face was blank. She didn't understand.

I tried again. "You're dead. You got hit when you were crossing a street a long time ago."

I waited for my words to sink in, but I wasn't entirely sure they would. Everything about this woman felt impatient. She wanted—*needed*—to keep moving. It was killing her to stop, stand still, and listen.

"You don't have to do this anymore."

My words still didn't seem to register.

"It's time to go," I said. "I can help you go somewhere else."

I could feel her exhaustion.

She never said a word, but she let me call in a bubble. I made sure to ask that the bubble of protection be filled with calming energy and peace that would offer her a better under-standing of her situation. This poor woman needed to rest.

She collapsed inside of it and let it take her to whatever was next.

A Murdered Night Watchman

There was once a ghost at the Palmer House who didn't know that he was dead. A night watchman had been shot out in the street, not far from the front entrance of the hotel. A psychic had been through the property and advised that everyone should just leave him alone. As long as he didn't know he was dead, he wouldn't be any trouble. However, she had warned, if he figured out he had been killed, there might be a problem.

While we knew about George's existence, we took the psychic's advice and steered clear of him. But one night, during an investigation for a Things That Go Bump event, John was in the basement when his head started to hurt. He felt a very agitated energy. It didn't take long for everyone to realize that George had figured out that he was dead.

Tuning in to the ghost's energy at the Palmer House, I knew that it was George, but I also knew he was incredibly confused and disoriented. He was trying to talk to John. He knew John was aware of his presence, so George would not leave him alone. It got to the point that John couldn't stay down in the basement because his head hurt so badly.

We were in the middle of a paranormal investigation event and had groups down there, so we weren't able to stop what we were doing and help George. In addition, Kelley had been warned about trying to help him before he was ready. I had a sense that in order to help him cross over, we needed to gather as much information as we could about his story first.

But we also couldn't let him try to mess with anyone else in the group. I connected to the higher self of the Palmer House and asked it to keep him safe and free of pain until we could come back to help him. In the meantime, I envisioned a bubble trying to wrap him up and hold him in a safe pod space. It didn't work—George didn't want to stay in it. His sense of urgency was too strong; his need to tell everyone what had happened to him was so pressing that it was his only focus.

Instead, I had to send a wall of energy down and through the hallway to keep him from coming into our space. It was one time where I've actually gotten a little nervous during something like this—I had a slight moment of doubt in myself and my abilities to keep everyone safe.

And then I remembered my inner-earth guide. I asked my Beetle Man guide to come stand next to me. Upon seeing my unusual guide next to me, the patrolman ghost was incredibly confused. I could feel him trying to figure out who or what my Beetle Man even was. That finally worked, and he left us alone after that. I tried my best to send him calming thoughts and reassure him that we would be back to help him out.

————————

When I got back to St. Paul, I went to the Minnesota Historical Society Library to see what I could find out. I really just wanted to find some information about his family. I was thinking that maybe a name would help me connect with someone who could come help him. What should have been a quick research assignment... wasn't.

The newspaper articles we were able to find about the situation were fascinating. They provided details about the entire situation. In 1929 a night patrolman, George Rosenberger, had been shot in the head in the early morning hours. His poor wife found him the next morning; she went out looking for him when he didn't show up for breakfast. He was lying in the street behind the police station, arms at his side, his pistol on the ground.

The coroner called for a jury to determine the cause of death. The newspaper article reported the three theories: suicide, accidental discharge of his firearm, and murder. The suicide theory was ruled out immediately because it would have been physically impossible for someone to shoot themselves in the way George had been shot. Also, he was said to be a happy person and had shown no signs of depression.

The article went on to report that the bullet found at the scene was inconsistent with the type he usually used in his firearm. In addition, for the bullet to accidentally fire from his weapon and hit him where it hit him, it would have had to ricochet off of the building, and no such mark was found in the brick wall. For all intents and purposes—even though the jury had yet to deliberate—based on the evidence presented, the newspaper article concluded that there was no other possibility but murder.

The next day, the newspaper reported that the jury had determined the cause of death was accidental discharge of a firearm.

With the help of a research librarian (I hate microfiche), I was able to find a copy of his death certificate. His name on the certificate was different than the name reported in the paper. I was fascinated by this until Kelley pointed out that in Sauk Centre, people rarely go by their given name. Being a small, traditional town, boys are often named after their fathers. It gets too confusing when everyone has the same name, so nicknames are common. But even so, finding out his real name would certainly help us help him.

I also learned that all of the coroner's inquest files from Stearns County had been sent to the history center library. I knew I had to try to pull George's file. I made a return trip just to look through that box. I sat patiently and waited for the big box of history to be delivered to my table, my anticipation and excitement growing.

As I flipped through the files, I realized there was a chunk missing. There was a gap in the records and of course, his file was in the gap. My mystery-writer/lawyer brain suspected it was no accident that his file was missing.

But in the long run, thanks to the thorough newspaper reporter, a lot of the details I would have found in the coroner's report and inquest transcript had already been reported in that long-ago article. We already had enough to suspect that he might have been murdered, and it might even have been covered up. But without the missing file, there would be no tangible way to prove any of it.

Some additional research about the town itself at the time revealed that it was a hot spot for bootleggers and illegal beer production during the peak of prohibition. If George had learned (through his position as night patrolman) about illegal bootlegging activities, it was a possible motive. Maybe he had been considered a disposable threat. In any event, we had enough information to help him get to where he needed to go now.

A few weeks later, we had a chance to help George in person. We were all meeting at the Palmer House on our way to Minnesota's Paracon. Paracon, an annual paranormal convention, was being held at a casino farther north. Kevin and I planned to go down to the basement. Chris (another friend and psychic) was also staying at the hotel and joined us in the basement. Mr. Rosenberger came right away when we called his name.

"We've figured out who you are," I explained. "We know justice wasn't served for you. But you don't have to worry anymore. We will take it from here and make sure your story is told."

I could feel him listening to us.

From across the room, Chris grabbed on to her head. "My head," she said. "Are you making my head hurt?"

"We know you got shot in the head," I said. "We know your head really hurts. But now you can go somewhere where it won't hurt anymore. You won't be in pain, and you'll have more clarity, and you'll even be able to come back and help us, if you want."

He finally felt ready to go.

But I knew that we needed to work discretely to protect the other energies in the building. It's almost like the soul of the Palmer House itself wanted to make sure no one else got upset.

Mentally, I called in my friend Mac. I asked him to walk George down the tunnel that sometimes appears for ghosts who are ready to leave the Palmer House.

"My friend is going to walk you through the tunnel," I said. "Your wife will be there waiting for you at the end of it."

Together, they walked off.

———

I believe that George came back again to see us not long after. He spoke through one of my favorite pieces of paranormal equipment, the Ovilus V. It's a device that was developed by paranormal equipment experts. The Ovilus was developed around the concept that spirits can manipulate energy to form words. This energy, via the Ovilus, can be translated using the device's internal database of preprogrammed words. It gets really interesting when words show up on the Ovilus that we know aren't in its dictionary—for example, a unique name or a word in another language. I like using the Ovilus in addition to other equipment as a way to help validate other evidence.

Once, I was telling a group of event participants about George. As I often do, I had an Ovilus V and a K2 meter operating next to me while I spoke to the group. In this case, the Ovilus began "talking" as I told the story about the murdered night watchman. It came up with the following words in this exact order: "clairvoyant," "murder," "certain," "result," "wrong," "am not," "around," "went," "release."

I will never know for sure if George was standing there next to me when I told his story in the café of the Palmer House, but the words that came through the Ovilus that day seemed to offer tangible evidence that he was.

Friday the Thirteenth at Paracon

I was thrilled to be invited to join the Palmer House group for Paracon. The Palmer House had been asked to present and had a booth at the convention. We arrived on Thursday afternoon in time for the VIP dinner. In the morning, we were up early because we had to set up our booth. When we went down for breakfast, the walkway to the restaurants and casino was blocked off and guarded by security guards. It was obvious something had happened, and whatever it was, it wasn't good.

The security guards routed us around the blocked off area, having us walk through the pool area to get to breakfast. My brain went through all of the reasons why they would have closed off the major walkway from the hotel rooms to the casino. I couldn't help coming up with potential scenarios; the mystery writer in me was curious. I imagined there had been a chemical spill of some kind and they were cleaning up. Or, more likely, they were having trouble with a guest who'd had too much to drink or something.

By the time we finished breakfast, the security staff had added a thick black curtain that stretched all the way across the walkway. The curtain was guarded by a security officer. My inner Nancy Drew was beyond curious. I was beginning to think that maybe someone had died.

Walking through the skyway back to the hotel room, I could see at least a dozen squad cars. I didn't need to see the coroner's van to know that someone had indeed died. I'd had enough experience with lawyers and the court system to know that with this amount of police presence, it probably hadn't been due to natural causes. *Although*, I thought, *maybe it was someone older who suffered a heart attack or stroke*. I found myself hoping that the story would turn out to be something like that.

I paused in the walkway that looked out over the parked squad cars and emergency vehicles. I sent a prayer of gratitude to all those who had responded for the work that they do. I also tried to send love to whoever the victim might have been.

I've always had a hard time with the chaotic energy in casinos and this one was no different. I work hard to keep my energy field locked and protected when I'm in one. The casino energy was already swirling together with all of the energy coming from the paranormal event itself—add in whatever tragedy that had just unfolded and this weekend was already shaping up to be intense.

An hour later, I was walking by and saw that the walkway was open again. At least now I knew that the suspicious death hadn't been a murder. A murder investigation would have required that the area be closed for a lot longer, most likely until the next day. I assumed that someone had had a heart attack.

Something deep inside me needed to know what happened. As a mystery writer, my curiosity and interest in mayhem is already beyond what is deemed normal. I'm a paranormal investigator, so my interest in death and what's going on with the other side of the veil only makes me even more strange. But this *need* to know was percolating from somewhere inside me … somewhere deeper than morbid curiosity.

It probably wasn't a coincidence that I had to go back to my room at the very same time the maids were in the hallway. I know enough about the metaphysical world to know that nothing is ever a coincidence. The maids were whispering with a woman who was dressed in a suit and carried herself with authority. She also had a radio attached her hip. It wasn't hard to deduce that she was a manager of some kind.

We had our "Do Not Disturb" sign on our door, but I wasn't going to miss an opportunity to get fresh towels, especially when it offered me an opportunity to start a conversation.

"Excuse me," I asked a maid. "I don't need service, but can I just take a few towels?"

"Sure," said the manager lady, giving me a stack and recording my room number on a clipboard hanging from the cart.

I put the towels in my room and came back into the hallway.

"I'm going to go back to my office," Manager Lady announced to the maids.

At the time I left my room, our paces matched exactly and I found myself walking right beside Manager Lady—another "coincidence." I realized this was exactly the way I would have written a scene for my character to find out information. Except... I would have ultimately deemed it too easy and not believable; I probably would've had to edit it in some way to make it less cliché. The universe had just presented me with an opportunity to get information about something I was worried about on some sort of soul level. I couldn't pass it up.

"It was quite an interesting morning," I said carefully, trying to start a conversation.

"What did you see?" she asked cautiously.

I thought it was interesting that she questioned me instead of simply agreeing. "When we were going down to breakfast, everything was blocked off and we had to walk through the pool area. Is everything okay?"

She nodded. "It's fine now."

I paused for a moment. "I write mystery novels, and the mystery writer in me has to know what happened. Did someone die?"

She studied me, no doubt noticing my giant "Presenter" badge.

"Mysteries? Like you buy in the bookstore?"

I nodded.

"That's really cool," she said.

I shrugged. "I hope that someday they are in a bookstore. They aren't there yet."

She nodded. "The person who died... it was a young woman," she said.

I felt like I'd been punched in my gut. I don't know what I'd been expecting; maybe I was still clinging to the thought that an older man or woman had a heart attack. But I hadn't expected to hear her say it was a young woman. I couldn't help but think that a young person meant it was probably a suicide.

"That's really terrible," I said, and meant it.

"I'm just glad that she was found by one of our employees and not a guest," she said.

"Was it in the lobby?" I asked. "We couldn't walk through when we went down to breakfast."

"No, she was in the women's restroom."

By this point, we were in the main building and I was really glad. It would have been strange to keep talking about it, but even more awkward to change the subject.

"I really hope your day gets better," I said.

She nodded and turned left down a hallway that looked like it went to an office area.

The main character in my mystery novel would have been proud of me for finding out more information. But this wasn't a mystery novel; this was real life. A young woman had died, from what was sure to have been something suspicious. My heart hurt for her.

———————

My friend Kevin doesn't travel anywhere without a variety of paranormal tools and investigative equipment. We were both invited to be part of the Palmer House team for Paracon and he had seen the police activity that morning as well. I found him and reported the information I'd learned. We spent the next few hours trying to deduce if there was an unsettled spirit who needed help.

Every time I tried to tune in to her energy, I felt chaos. But I couldn't be entirely sure if I was just picking up on the general chaotic energy of the casino combined with the energy of Paracon.

The more I thought about it, the more it began to feel like it had been a suicide. But now that I knew it was a young woman, I wasn't sure if my logical brain was just projecting what I was expecting it to be. I also noticed that whenever I thought about her, I got a huge cramp in my abdomen. I started to wonder if maybe she had been pregnant.

Later, we happened to be on that side of the building for a break. I wanted to try to separate her energy from the rest of the chaotic energy coming from every direction in the casino. There was only one place I could think to do that. I gathered up my courage and went into the only women's restroom that was in the corridor that had been blocked off by the police that morning.

When I walked in, I immediately felt an aversion to the last stall—the larger handicapped one—and nothing in this physical world could have convinced me to push through that door. Instead, I went into the stall next to it and shut the door. I knew I'd found her energy. It was definitely unsettled and chaotic, amplified by the darker energy of the casino. But in that moment, it also felt impossible to do anything to help her. I had to walk out, knowing there was nothing I could do.

Not long after, we were backstage waiting to go on for our presentation. I should have been thinking about our panel presentation. I should have been thinking about what the heck I was going to say if anyone asked a question about the ghosts at the Palmer House and I suddenly ended up in the spotlight. But my thoughts were still with the poor girl who had died. I found myself eavesdropping on employees talking, whispering and consoling each other. I wanted to tell them how sorry I was that a tragedy like that had been a part of their day. I thought about how strange it was to have the convention happening as planned when the day began as anything but normal for this staff.

We were standing with our handler, who worked for both the convention and the casino. We were all just making small talk anyway, so I figured it wouldn't hurt to ask him if he knew anything about the girl I couldn't seem to get out of my mind.

"You don't have to tell me anything, and if I'm out of line for asking, please don't feel like you have to answer."

He narrowed his eyes at me.

"What happened this morning? I know it was a young woman, and I know it happened in the restroom." I rushed to explain, before I lost my courage.

"You know all of that?" he asked, clearly impressed.

I shrugged. "I talked to the maids," I explained. "The maids always know everything." I wasn't about to tell him I was psychic. I still wasn't comfortable admitting that to complete strangers.

"It was a drug overdose," he said.

A puzzle piece clicked into place. That explained why everything around her energy felt confused and chaotic. And given all of the other circumstances, I probably should have figured that out before this.

"She actually did the same thing the night before too," he continued. "They found her yesterday too, the same way. She was unconscious, but she was still alive. They sent her to the hospital."

That explained why I was feeling like it was suicidal. Her overdose had seemed to be very intentional. "That's terrible," I said, feeling an intense rush of empathy for this poor girl.

"They must have released her and sent her home. Because she came back again, only to do the exact same thing. But this time, she didn't make it."

After this conversation, my guides stepped in on my behalf. After verifying the victim was a young woman and the circumstances surrounding her death, my perspective shifted. Some of the empathic pain I'd been experiencing lifted. My analysis became more objective. My guides stepped in to help keep me moving in the right direction ... which was all about making sure this poor soul got help.

———————

A few hours later, I got a text from Kevin. "Do you think she is at peace?" he asked. I had talked to him earlier in the day about what I'd learned.

His question echoed everything that had been circling through my head all day. I was pretty sure I knew the answer.

Both convention rooms were packed with people. Around me, people everywhere were enjoying their day immersed in all things paranormal. Our own booth had lines of people waiting to talk to Kelley, ask questions about the Palmer House, and purchase merchandise. But we had enough of us that we were taking turns. So instead of answering Kevin's text, I went to find him.

"Isn't it interesting," I said when I found him, "that we are at a convention filled with psychics and paranormal investigators, and no one else even seems to notice that something happened?"

Kevin shrugged. "That's probably not a bad thing. We don't need everyone trying to bother this poor girl."

Later that day, Kevin and I were talking about it again. Kelley came to sit with us. "Is it the bathroom on the way to the lobby?" she asked.

"Yes," I said. "Why?"

"I was just in there, all by myself. When I was washing my hands, I looked at myself in the mirror and I could see a thin girl standing behind me."

Kevin and I looked at each other.

"Should we take some equipment in there? We can try to confirm she's still there and get some evidence?" he asked.

"By 'we'... do you really mean 'me'? Considering it's the ladies' restroom?" I asked.

Kevin laughed. "I guess you're right."

I already *knew* she was there, but it never hurt to have physical evidence, especially for my logical lawyer brain. And because the energy in the whole casino at this convention was so chaotic, it would be nice to verify anything we could.

Kevin went back to his room to get a few pieces of equipment. Considering only one of us was going to get into the women's restroom, he handed me a K2 meter (a K2 meter measures electromagnetic energy) and an Ovilus; he knows it's my favorite piece of ghost-hunting equipment.

He also tried to give me a voice recorder. I handed it right back. "You probably don't want to record everyone peeing."

"Good point," he said with a laugh.

The Ovilus wasn't working, so all I ended up with was a K2 meter. But by now the bathroom was crowded, and I couldn't exactly walk around to do a baseline sweep. Women all around me were talking about the autographs they'd gotten, the readings they'd had done, or the rocks they'd purchased. It was too difficult to discern whose energy belonged to who.

Later that day, I walked by the restroom and noticed a large yellow sign braced in the doorframe to block it for maintenance and cleaning. I texted Kevin: "If I were writing a mystery novel, my main character would steal the bathroom 'closed for service sign' so that you would be able to sneak into the women's restroom."

But it was real life. Someone had really died, and I wasn't as brave as my main character would have been.

The next morning, I went down to get coffee and found myself walking by the women's restroom. I felt an overwhelming need to go inside, like the young woman was finally ready to go. My arms were filled with bags and everything I would need for the day. Instead of trying to manage all of that in the restroom, I went to our booth where I knew I'd be by myself. It would be easier to check in remotely and without interruption, especially since the exhibit halls hadn't opened yet.

Once inside the vendor area, I was stopped by two friends. "Did you hear there was a suspicious death here yesterday?"

I nodded but didn't want to talk about it. Word had gotten out, rumors were starting to spread, and it was time to make sure this poor girl could find her way to heaven.

I sat quietly in our corner and closed my eyes. I could see her standing there, thin and frail. I could feel her desperation. I asked my crew what she needed. They told me all she needed was to see angels. Just for good measure, Mary came as well. She took her by the hand and they went off together.

For the rest of the day, we listened to rumors about the mysterious Friday the thirteenth death at Paracon.

None of the stories got it right.

———————

I have since heard about other lightworkers at Paracon doing work to help her. This makes sense to me. It makes sense that her guides and angels would have been reaching out to a wide pool of people who might be able to help her. She needed help, and there were a lot of people who were capable and in the right place at the right time with the availability to help. There were probably a lot of us working together without even realizing it.

Is This Heaven?

In Minnesota, winters are brutal. As soccer players, my boys often play in a Minneapolis indoor futsal league (a version of soccer played on a basketball court). They also signed up for a six-week training league on Saturday mornings. Any time they can sign up for the same activity at the same time, it is a bonus for me—it means less driving!

Saturday mornings, we fell into a routine. I would take them to their futsal workshop at the YWCA, just over the Mississippi

River in Minneapolis. I would run around the indoor track while they played. I'm a wimp when it comes to running outside in the winter in Minnesota. I also haven't been back on a treadmill since the hotel gym incident—I am not about to start any time soon.

Our Saturday morning route across the Mississippi River and into Minneapolis was peaceful and usually devoid of other cars. This neighborhood used to be very different. When I was in college (about twenty years ago), it was a street we avoided. Even if there was a sober driver and everyone wanted tacos from the twenty-four-hour Taco Bell, we would think really hard about venturing across the river bridge and heading more than four or five blocks into Minneapolis. During my senior year of college, I volunteered at a shelter for kids in the heart of this neighborhood. It was a place where drive-by shootings were common and no man or woman should have walked alone.

Now, it was lighter and much more peaceful. The demographics of the neighborhood shifted. Most storefronts have removed the heavy iron bars that used to adorn their windows. The twenty-four-hour Taco Bell has been turned into a Tim Hortons. Graffiti has been scrubbed from walls and cute shops and restaurants have opened—some even feature patios. But there is still a residual current of energy, leftover from the days of street gang violence, that still seems to cycle through.

Perhaps that current of energy is what prompted my two boys to invent their game Haunted or Not Haunted. We usually get about two or three blocks over the Mississippi River when one of them suggests we play. It's quite easy—they point to a building and I have to say if it's haunted or not. We've played enough times where now, instead of me answering every question, I make them answer too. It's the only route we've ever driven where they suggest playing it.

———————

I was hired to clear a house. This client came to me through a social media post. She had posted something about having a paranormal experience and someone tagged me in the post to help explain what might be going on.

She had been home alone in her house. She said that she was walking down the hallway and suddenly felt as though she were seeing a scene that happened in the house a few years before. The pizza cutter in her hand wasn't really a pizza cutter, but a knife. She was hearing intruders downstairs, but she knew they weren't really there. I invited her to PM me her address so I could do a remote scan to see if anything was there.

She shared a few more details with me. The previous owner of the home had been murdered during a break-in. He'd been living there with his fiancée at the time. She knew the family and the history of the home. It hadn't prevented her from moving in. Instead, she felt like she could help the house in some way by living in it.

I looked up the address and was shocked when I realized where her house was located. She lived on the Minneapolis side of the Mississippi River, just a block off of the route I drove every Saturday morning. It was exactly the point in our route where my boys always suggest playing our Haunted or Not Haunted game.

I tuned in. Her cute little house definitely fell into the former of the two categories. I dug a little deeper and tried to find a newspaper article about the murder. I don't usually do additional research for my client's properties before I go in to do a clearing. If anything, I might research a property after I've finished in order to find validating evidence of something I picked up on when I was in the house. But in this case, I felt a compelling need to know more before I began.

I wasn't prepared for the chills that rushed through my body as I read. The owner of the house was a graduate of the same college my husband went to, as well as my husband's best friend Mac, who was now a member of my dead crew. The article reported that someone broke into this home in the middle of the night. That's exactly what had happened with Mac. The owner was upstairs and, while his fiancée hid, he went down to face the intruders, armed with a knife. The intruders were members of a street gang with the wrong address—they were looking for a house nearby known to have drugs.

The situation was eerily similar to what had happened to Mac. Mac had been asleep in his room in the basement when he heard a noise and went to investigate. He surprised an intruder breaking into the kitchen. Police suspected the perpetrator was a member of a street gang looking for drugs.

Both young men were shot in the abdomen and died shortly thereafter. The biggest difference between the two stories was that this man's murderers were caught and convicted, while Mac's case has long since been declared "cold."

I tuned in again. Mac grinned at me immediately. "This one is for me," he said.

"No problem," I answered.

I tuned in to the energy of the young man. I was overwhelmed with feelings of sadness, but also relief. He was very confused. It seemed like he had just realized he was dead. He knew he was in his home, but everything was the wrong color. He was showing me the white walls. He had realized someone else was living in his home and he was confused.

I asked him to tell me something that would help the new owner believe me when I explained to her that I had talked to him.

He said, "There are two boys."

He was already ready to go. It was as if his confusion lifted just by seeing Mac. He knew that Mac was ready to take him wherever he was supposed to go. They walked off together, arm in arm—two comrades who had only just met, both who had lived lives that were stolen much too soon.

I checked back in with my client to tell her what had happened.

"He was really confused about the colors in the house. He recognized the house as his, but couldn't understand why the colors were different."

My client explained that the house had been redone. For me, that explained a lot. He had realized the house was familiar, but he was so confused because it was different than it had been when he'd been living in it.

"He also said something about two boys," I said. "Did he have two boys? Or maybe two nephews?"

She gasped. "I have two little boys," she said.

After this case, others started to come fast and furious. It began to feel like I had a whole stack of files waiting for me. As soon as I would finish one, another would show up to take its place. But for all Mac has done for me, I was glad that this one landed on our desk.

TEN

EMOTIONAL HAZARDS

Author's Note: Out of respect for the individuals involved, identifying details such as where this story took place and who was involved have been removed. I had to include this story, even in its stripped-down version. It weighed heavily on me for days. It was the first time I realized this new job of mine came with a hazard I hadn't been expecting. I'm mostly able to stay emotionally detached from the souls I am helping, but this one hurt my heart and rattled me to my core.

One weekend I was with a friend as they got the news that someone they knew had passed unexpectedly. In the days leading up to this, there had been signs that they would need a little extra help. I can't share them because I want to protect the family's privacy. But the wisdom of hindsight revealed that it was almost as if the universe was booking an appointment with people who would be able to help, knowing what was coming around the corner.

It was a sudden death, completely and totally unexpected and out of the blue. It was the kind of news that punches hard in the gut. There was no possible way to have seen it coming. It was a tragedy by every definition of the word: she was a mother who was taken suddenly, leaving her family behind.

Those of us who were there to look back and put the clues together checked in with her spirit after she died. Her spirit was unsettled, upset, and really angry. We realized immediately that there was nothing any of us could do in that moment. Over the next couple of days, I tried to check in with her, but couldn't. It was almost like I couldn't even find her.

A few days went by. One afternoon I checked in again. I still couldn't do anything to help, but this time, I seemed to be able to get a message across. I told her that if she needed my help in any way, I would be there for her.

About an hour later I was hit with overwhelming sadness. It came out of nowhere and I knew it wasn't mine. But it was so strong, powerful, and concerning that I worried about people close to me. I checked in with everyone in my family. At one point, I even texted my friend Jessica to make sure everything was okay.

And then I realized it was coming from her—the poor mother who had been taken from this world so young. Her soul was having a difficult time accepting that her life on this earth was done. She was exhausted and ready to accept some help.

Normally, I'm protected from those rushes of emotions that aren't mine. In this case, I knew my guides had intentionally let it through to affect me. It got my attention and forced me to stop what I was doing in my routine daily life so I could figure out where it was coming from.

It was the middle of the afternoon on an extremely busy day, but I knew I had to make time to check in. I was running kids home from school, over to the skating rink, and back to school again to get the kid who had a student council meeting. I got him home and reminded the boys they had to get ready for soccer practice. Then I stuffed my quartz crystal and my favorite chunk of amethyst into my pocket and hurried back to the rink to wait for my skater girl to finish. I had approximately twenty-four minutes before her lesson ended. After that, I would have to leave and do another route—get the skater home and start the soccer carpool pickup.

Fishing my rocks out of my pocket, I clutched the quartz in my right hand, the amethyst in my left, and went up into the stands. I tried to find a corner where I could sit and close my eyes but it would look like I was watching the skaters on the ice. I had just closed my eyes to begin to tap in, when a friend (a real-life living, breathing human) came to sit next me to watch her daughter.

My guides are used to this happening. My kids walk in on me all of the time when I am trying to do remote work, or they'll start fighting and I have to yell at them to be quiet. The irony of that is not lost on me—finding a quiet moment to sit and help a spirit find peace, only to have to stop and yell at my kids.

When anything like this happens, my guides simply step back and wait until I deal with the real-life moment that interrupted me. In this case, my friend was busy watching her daughter so it was easy to excuse myself. I went to find a different quiet corner, which isn't always easy at the skating rink. I settled into a chair off in a corner on the opposite side of the rink.

The first image I had of this woman showed me how much she was stuck. My guides showed me mud and I interpreted that literally. She was stuck in the mud and heaviness of an in-between dimension. And now she was also exhausted. Her spirit was so tired of fighting the inevitable. She absolutely did not want to leave her physical body behind and join the spirit world because in doing so, she thought she would be leaving her beloved family behind.

She looked at me, and her sadness and grief was overwhelming. She pleaded with me to help her stay—something I knew was completely out of my control, not to mention impossible. I tried to explain that if she went with the angels, she could come back and be with her family forever and always. She would be at a higher vibration and better able to help them. Suddenly, there was a whole team of angels behind me. She finally agreed to leave with them, and one of them scooped her up and carried her off in his arms.

For the rest of the evening, any time I thought of her it came with the same overwhelming sadness I'd felt earlier in the day. It overcame me to the point of tears. I sobbed uncontrollably for a good fifteen minutes. The song "In the Arms of an Angel" by Sarah McLachlan ran through my head for the rest of the week and I broke down and cried every time it did. I'm usually a really strong person, so I wasn't used to falling to pieces quite so easily. But it almost felt like a purge—one that wasn't even mine. I seemed to be purging the grief she felt about dying on her behalf. It was as if she needed someone to hold her grief and carry it for her in order to move on to the next world.

My guides allowed it in, which meant that I could handle it. Ultimately, I was happy to be able to give her that gift. But this experience led me to acknowledge a job hazard and side effect of this gift that I'd never even thought about—the emotional trauma I would sometimes be called to carry.

Baby Girl

About two weeks before the 2018 Super Bowl, someone I only know on social media (who lives in a completely different part of the country) shared a photo of a missing person who was a friend of a friend. I looked at the photo of the missing girl and got an instant download of information that chilled me to my core. The download told me she had been abducted by a sex-trafficking ring and was going to be shipped to Minnesota as a response to the increased demand brought on by the Super Bowl.

Within five minutes of this download, I convinced myself that I was crazy and overacting. My logical brain had obviously made note of all of the fear-inducing articles about watching for signs of sex trafficking in Minneapolis during the Super Bowl. People I knew had been sharing all kinds of fear-based lists and warnings on social media for weeks. I concluded that my mystery-writer brain had obviously filled in the gaps to set up the perfect crime.

But I couldn't shake the feeling that in spite of all the work my logical brain was doing to try to talk me out of my theory, I was right. Every time I looked at her photo, I got the same gut feeling. My gut feelings aren't usually wrong. By this point, the researcher in me had pulled articles about her disappearance to gather more details. She'd been seen with someone suspicious after she had disappeared. This was apparently someone she'd met online. But she'd left a suicide note.

My mystery-writer-self argued that it would be a brilliant way to disappear and throw anyone off the scent. My gut agreed that the suicide note was staged.

By the end of the week, my gut was screaming louder than it had ever screamed before. The only possible relief was to try to tune in to the situation the same way I do any sort of remote work and see what I could get.

I could see her in a warehouse. I knew it was just outside of Chicago. She was heavily drugged and had been passed off to others and was already deep within "the system." That's what my guides called it, "the system." I knew that in the next day or two, she'd be on her way to Minneapolis. It felt like the first few days she'd be in an inner suburb, probably Eden Prairie or Bloomington. But my information said that by the weekend, she'd be in a swanky hotel in Minneapolis.

I shouted at her. "Wake up, get out!"

She looked at me, her eyes hazy and confused. "You're strong enough to survive this," I told her. "You can get out of this."

And then I saw her grandmother. Her grandmother, who had passed, was the reason I'd been pulled in to help with this case. She somehow seemed to know to come find me.

There wasn't much I could do in that moment. I shouted at her a little more and tried to wrap her up in whatever protection my angels could come up with. I knew she'd have angels with her throughout her ordeal. I knew her guides and grandmother would be helping her try to escape.

But I had to do something more. I looked online. All of the websites were general and vague. There was no number to call with "psychic information." I laughed at myself. Of course there wasn't a hotline I could call. I had nothing tangible to go on. I couldn't call a general hotline number and tell them I'd had a "vision."

But then I remembered a mom I had met at the pool last summer. Our kids are at the same school and we always found ourselves sitting together in the afternoon outings to the pool. She was a police officer for the city of Minneapolis. She knew I wrote ghost stories. She had no idea I was psychic.

I still had her number in my phone. I sat and looked at my phone for several minutes trying to gather the courage to call. When I finally dialed, the call went to voicemail and I had to leave a message.

"Hi…" I began. I reminded her who I was, then said, "I have a really strange question about a missing person's case. If you have time at all, could you give me a call?"

I'd done all I could for the moment. It was out of my hands. She called back within five minutes.

"I'm just finishing my shift," she explained. "What's up?"

"I know you know I write ghost stories," I explained. "But I've also figured out that I'm really psychic." I continued without waiting for a response because I didn't want to lose my nerve. "I have no idea where you fall on that, but I don't know who else to talk to. Usually, I help dead people. This is the first time I've ever gotten psychic information about someone who is still alive and I don't know what to do about it."

I went on to tell her what I knew and what I'd seen. And no matter how hard I tried, I couldn't seem to do it without crying. It felt so urgent, and I have never felt more helpless. It was such a relief to be telling someone something. And yet, I was still terrified to tell anyone else about my gifts. I was so afraid of being judged.

She was incredibly kind. "I believe in that gut feeling," she said. "It's what I tell my kids—or any kids I'm coaching—to listen to. There's something to that. I am sure that some people have those senses stronger than others."

Relief flooded through me.

"For this," she said. "We would need something specific. You are not wrong that the sex trafficking has increased because of the Super Bowl. We are doing raids all the time. We just did another one yesterday. We just need something specific. If you sense that she's in Minneapolis and you can get me something specific, I'll see what I can do."

"Okay," I agreed, thanking her profusely. It felt good to have a plan.

That same weekend, I happened to spend time with a friend who does intelligence work for a number of different agencies. In my work, I don't believe in coincidences. I told her the story.

"I have access to the Back Pages," she said.

"What are the Back Pages?"

"You don't want to know," she said. "But if you can come up with a name that they might be using for her, I can check to see if she's there. I have a friend who is assigned to the special task force for Super Bowl sex trafficking."

———————

The day of the Super Bowl drew closer. I tried to tune in. I wondered if I should just drive up and down the streets of downtown Minneapolis to see if I got a hit or feeling about a location. But subjecting myself to the icky energy radiating from everything having to do with the Super Bowl was the last thing I wanted to do.

Instead, I focused on trying to find her new name. The name "Katie" kept popping in my head. I tuned in and connected with her energy. I sat with my notebook, ready to brainstorm any name that came to mind. If my friend could search one name, she could search several.

I asked her what name they were using for her.

"Baby Girl" was what they called her. That's all she could give me.

Of course. How would she possibly know what name they were using for her online?

First, I wrote down the name "Katie" because it had been popping in my head all week. And as soon as I saw the letters on the page, I knew I had spelled it wrong.

"Spell it with a 'y,'" said a voice inside my head. It was her grandmother.

So I wrote "Katy" with a "y." That was the only name I had to give my friend to search.

By then it was Super Bowl weekend, and I felt an odd sense of calm. I had done everything I could do. I did not drive the streets of Minneapolis; it was all I could do to even have the television on during the big game.

Nothing came of it and no leads popped up. The flow of information stopped and again, all I felt was a bizarre sense of calm and peace. A few weeks went by. Another social media post popped up, shared by the same friend-of-a-friend. It read "RIP" and showed the photo of the girl I'd been trying to help for the last several weeks. My heart sank.

I clicked around until I could find the newspaper articles. Her body had been found not far from where she had disappeared. She was found in the water.

The mystery writer in me realized that if her story had played out the way I saw it in my head, this was the perfect crime. She was needed for the increased demand. But she was a liability because there were a lot of people looking for her. I was also pretty sure she was feisty and not the easiest to control. It was easy to bring her back to the spot where she'd already written a fake suicide note. In fact, it may have been the plan all along. In addition, if she were dumped in the water in the middle of winter, it would presumably take a while (longer than this) to find her body, thus making the time of her death difficult to determine. Not to mention, any evidence of sexual assault would be long gone.

The end of the article asked anyone with any information to call the homicide department, leaving me to believe that perhaps they thought her death was suspicious. I wondered what would happen if someone with psychic information called that number. I didn't know if I was brave enough to call a homicide department in another state and give them my download of psychic information. Having been a lawyer, I wondered if that would give me any credibility. Lawyers don't always have the greatest reputation.

But when it came right down to it, I chose not to base my decision on what anyone would think about me, but rather what I would be able to live with for myself. I realized I would regret it if I didn't say anything. If I had information that could possibly help solve a crime—a murder—I needed to speak up.

I also observed how emotionally detached I was from the outcome. At this point, it was all about me doing whatever I needed to do so I could move forward without regret. In that moment, I wasn't emotional about her or what had happened to her, it was just about having information to share. I called and left a message for the homicide detective assigned to the case.

She called me back first thing the next morning. I waited until I dropped my kids off at school, then pulled over to the side of the road and dialed her number. With each ring, my heart beat louder and harder until it was practically in my throat.

When she answered, I started right in. "I've never done anything like this before in my life. I used to be a lawyer, but now I'm a psychic medium. I might have some information about one of your cases."

I explained how I saw a post on social media that triggered several downloads of information. "Usually," I explained, "I help dead people. This is the first time I've ever had information about someone who was still alive."

"Well, actually . . ." she said.

But I interrupted. If I was going to do this, I had to say everything all at once before I lost my nerve. "I think that she was needed for the increased demand for the sex-trafficking trade. I'm in Minneapolis, and I feel like she was here." I described everything I felt and "saw" over the last several weeks.

"I know you found her, and I just wanted to share what I got, just in case it mattered in any way."

"Thank you," she said. "I really appreciate you taking the time to call. But actually . . ." She paused as if she weren't sure if she should share anything with me. "We're fairly convinced it was a suicide."

Her words punched me in the gut.

"Okay," I said, feeling ridiculous. "Thanks for your time. I'm so sorry to bother you."

"It's not a bother at all," she said and hung up.

I sat in the car for a few minutes processing her words and the information she shared. I realized there was a little voice inside my head that still disagreed with what she told me. *They didn't check*, said that voice. *They are wrong.*

This thought grew louder over the next few days.

Ultimately, there was nothing I could do about it, nor was there anything I felt like I was supposed to do about it. It wasn't my fight to fight. It was just about me speaking up and giving them something else to think about.

There will never be a way to confirm if any of the information I got through my psychic senses was right. According to that homicide detective, it was not. But according to everything I've ever been guided toward with my gift thus far … it was.

About a week later, "Baby Girl" showed up for me. I wasn't thinking about her but suddenly, there she was. She was dressed all in white, in a flowing, beautiful dress. She had flowers in her hair and a smile on her face. Her smile calmed me. No matter what had happened, I knew without a doubt that she was safe and her spirit was at peace. And that was enough for me.

ELEVEN
UNEXPECTED ENDINGS

A few months ago, I got some shocking news in the form of a social media post. One of my favorite restaurants, Forepaugh's, had closed without notice. I have celiac disease, and it was the only place I'd ever been that had gluten-free cheese curds on their menu. But more important, Forepaugh's was also home to some of my favorite ghosts of all time.

I got in touch with the managers right away to let them know I was thinking about them. They certainly didn't owe me any answers or an explanation—I knew they were busy handling all of the things that happen when a restaurant suddenly closes without much notice. I volunteered to be there at a moment's notice if the managers needed help with the "other side" of the Forepaugh's staff.

About a week later, I got a message: "We want to say goodbye." Kevin, Jessica, and I made arrangements to meet with the managers, Mimi and Joe, on one of their last days in the building. The whole day leading up to our meeting was filled with overwhelming feelings of anxiety and sadness that I knew were not my own. The ghosts were upset.

I mentally prepared myself for a long night of work. If the ghosts were ready to go to where they were supposed to go all along, I wanted to be ready to help them. I fully expected to walk into the old, beautiful house ready to help whichever souls were ready to cross over.

We met in the parlor, my favorite room in the house. It's the room where we caught images of ghosts on the SLS camera. It's the room where an elderly female ghost, who used to live in the building, sits in the front window. It's the room where my oldest son sat and ate a cheeseburger and proceeded to describe all of the ghosts on the second floor—the most notable being the late Governor Ramsey. I will never forget the look on his face when I pulled up a photo of Governor Ramsey and he realized it was the ghost he was describing. The parlor—and the whole house—carried so many memories.

My heart was heavy as we walked through the house. We started down in the basement kitchen and worked our way upstairs to the top floor. The sadness was palpable. When we got to the third floor, we all sat down at different tables. They were still set for diners who would never come, in what is known as "Molly's room." Every ghost in the building was gathered there with us.

Those of us in the living world talked for a while. We talked about the book signing we'd done several years before. We told stories about our investigations. We talked about how much we loved the building and everyone and everything in it. At times,

I started to cry. But even though I was feeling sad, I knew it wasn't so much *my* sadness that was bringing me to tears, but theirs.

After a while, we explained to the ghosts what was happening. They, of course, already knew. I offered to help anyone who wanted it. I explained that they all had freewill choice and they didn't have to stay in this house, or in this dimension, if they didn't want to.

When I said that, I got an image in my head. There were several ghosts, all standing together, wearing clothes from different eras and time periods. For some of them, it would have been impossible for them to know each other in real life because they hadn't existed in the same time and space until after. Despite all of their differences, I knew from a deep place of knowing that they had already agreed that no matter what, they were sticking together.

If one wanted to go, they would all go. I felt the three little boys thinking about it. They peeked out from behind an older gentleman's suit. I felt another ghost promise to take care of them if they stayed.

It felt like a scene out of a musical. It felt as if they were about to all link arms together and start singing a song about sticking together. It would be accompanied by a perfectly choreographed dance—just like something out of *Les Misérables*.

But at the end of it all, the decision had been made: they were going to stick it out and see what was going to happen next. They had decided to stay. I told them that they would know how to find me if they changed their minds.

And then we said goodbye.

Freewill choice is a powerful thing.

Full Circle

It had been a crazy summer and our busy family hadn't been in the same place at the same time much at all. If it wasn't a work trip for my husband, it was an event for me. If it wasn't a soccer tournament for one of the boys, it was a skating competition for Isabelle. One Wednesday night, we realized no one had anything and we would all be home at the same time for dinner. That was reason enough to go out for burgers.

At dinner I got a text message from my friend Melissa, who had taken some of my classes. It said, "I think I have a portal in my house. My daughter has been telling me for a while now that she feels like someone is always watching her. Especially upstairs. Every now and then, I feel a lower-vibrational presence. In fact, I'm pretty sure it's sitting on my feet right now."

I considered how, over the course of the last year, my text messages have gotten a lot more exciting. I looked at the bottle of beer in my hand (my second) and texted back, promising to scan her house first thing in the morning. (I never work when I've been drinking.)

The next morning, I woke up and could barely move. Earlier in the week I had somehow pulled a muscle in my back, and I practically had to crawl down the hallway after I got up. Fortunately for me, I was able to get an appointment with my chiropractor right away in the morning. Unfortunately for

Melissa, this meant I couldn't check in on her house right away like I'd promised.

The day continued with all of the craziness that a summer day with three busy kids usually brings. Fortunately, it was a Thursday, which meant it was an office day for me. I knew that I would be able to drop my daughter off at the skating rink and sneak away to my office for a little peace and quiet.

When I got there, the first thing on my list was to tune in to Melissa's house. Before I even began, I could sense the male presence she was referring to. My dead crew also told me that she did have a portal somewhere in the house, but this time it wasn't a mirror.

As I tuned in, I got an image in my head. The man—barely a man—was about seventeen or eighteen years old, and he had a gun in his hand. I could sense his fear. His unsettled soul had never, in his entire life, known what it felt like to feel safe. My download told me that he was a victim of gun violence and had died by his own hand or another—probably a combination of both. He had killed and he had been killed.

I usually don't see a ghost's face as clearly as I saw his. His dark eyes held a sadness—his life on this earth had been a tough one. He had found his way into Melissa's house through a portal in the attic. He had stayed in her house because she was a good mom. And in her house, he felt safer than he'd ever felt in his life.

But he also had learned that Melissa's family could sense his anxiousness. He could feel the fear from Melissa's daughter and had realized that fear could fuel him. He wasn't planning on going anywhere.

By this point, I usually have some idea of what a spirit needs to see or hear to move on. But this time, I had nothing. I reached out my hand to this young man, and he held it. His eyes met mine and I knew he felt safe holding it. Next, I gave him a hug and could feel that he felt even safer.

"You can go somewhere where you feel safe all of the time," I explained.

I still didn't get any sense of what I should do next. This was really unusual for me. I hadn't gotten a download of who or what he needed to see.

I decided to fall back on calling in a helper. I thought of Mac.

He was there instantly. As soon as I saw him, I realized my mistake. Mac had been murdered. While his case had never been solved, it had always been suspected that he had been killed by a gang member who had broken into his house—someone just like the ghost standing in front of me.

"Oh my God," I said. "I didn't realize. Maybe you weren't the right person to call."

Mac got a big grin on his face.

"Don't worry about it," he said. "Unconditional love and acceptance, right? Forgiveness? We all need forgiveness."

He put his arm around the kid and they went off together.

"I was exactly the right person to call," he said as he walked away.

When it was all over, I sat in my office and sobbed.

I cried because our world is so messed up that we kill each other with guns. I cried because Mac could be so accepting and forgiving even though his life that had been stolen by a gun. I cried because my physical body wasn't capable of handling the wave and vibration of unconditional love that I had just experienced.

And then I headed back to the skating rink to pick up my daughter so we could go home and make dinner.

EPILOGUE

I was told over and over again throughout my childhood, "There is no such thing as ghosts. It's just your imagination." I spent a long time second-guessing myself and my gifts because of it. But now, because of the work that I do and the people and souls that I help, I know and understand something different.

Sometimes the spirits that we feel around us *have* gone to heaven. Part of their heaven might be coming back to check on us. In my experience, heaven can be a lot closer than we realize. I hope this book helps people see that and find comfort. Our loved ones are never really gone. They can be with us in a moment if we just ask.

Sometimes souls get stuck. There *is* such a thing as ghosts. They can be the stuck souls who died with chaos, confusion, anger, or hate and somehow missed their white light. They can be the stuck souls who, by their own freewill choice, chose to stay in this world for some reason. Regardless, these small slivers of souls that used to be walking, talking, breathing human beings are stuck in the nether—somewhere between this dimension and the one they were supposed to go to all along.

Some of us can see, feel, sense, and know that they are there. Children now are especially sensitive to ghosts and spirit energy. They are being born with intuitive gifts like never before. It's almost like we are watching evolution happen right before our eyes.

I am trying to teach my own children better than I was taught. My children will never hear me say that the dark shadow is "just their imagination" or that there is "no such thing" as ghosts. They will always hear me say, "You don't have to be afraid of it." They will also hear me remind them that they are in charge of their own energy fields. They can choose what they let in (light and love) and they can block out what they don't want (the emotions of others). Being an empath is a gift; it doesn't have to be a curse.

My interest in ghosts and my involvement in the paranormal community has had a unique evolution. My Ghost Stories Ink group explores the paranormal as a way to find inspiration from the dark depths of history, allowing the past to seep into the present through a good ghost story.

But it also inspired me to do and look for more. As new advancements are made in technology and science, and quantum physics begins to catch up to better explain some of what I've experienced, I am excited to see how the paranormal community evolves.

Kevin, my colleague and co-founder of Paranormal Services Cooperative, once said, "If you took all of the paranormal evidence we've gathered over the course of the last year and presented everything to a judge or jury, we would be able to prove—beyond a reasonable doubt—that something else is there. We are interacting with an intelligent energy."

If we know that something is there, the next question becomes, "What the heck are we supposed to do about it?" I want to help people answer that question. No child should be afraid to sleep in their own room. No homeowner should be afraid to walk through the front door of their own home.

Likewise, no lost soul or ghost should have to spend all eternity existing in the nether and trying to get the attention of the living. They shouldn't have to lurk around looking for a boost of energy through someone else's fear. They should be able to go to the place where they were meant to go all along. Every lost soul deserves to be rescued.

Over the years, spirits have taught me a lot about myself, my gifts, and the world beyond.

I am a better person because of every single one of the ghosts I have met.

To Write to the Author

If you wish to contact the author or would like more information about this book, please write to the author in care of Llewellyn Worldwide Ltd. and we will forward your request. Both the author and publisher appreciate hearing from you and learning of your enjoyment of this book and how it has helped you. Llewellyn Worldwide Ltd. cannot guarantee that every letter written to the author can be answered, but all will be forwarded. Please write to:

Natalie Fowler
% Llewellyn Worldwide
2143 Wooddale Drive
Woodbury, MN 55125-2989

Please enclose a self-addressed stamped envelope for reply,
or $1.00 to cover costs. If outside the U.S.A., enclose
an international postal reply coupon.

Many of Llewellyn's authors have websites with additional information and resources. For more information, please visit our website at http://www.llewellyn.com.